An Illustrated History of Roundhay Park

by
Steven Burt

No intelligent person, ever visits any place of interest, either in search for health
or to give another fillip to a constitution already robust, without desiring, in addition
to the pleasure of beautiful scenery and a pure bracing atmosphere,
some information as to the history and associations attaching to the place
he has chosen to visit.

Charles Goodall's 'Illustrated Royal Handbook to Roundhay Park', September 1872

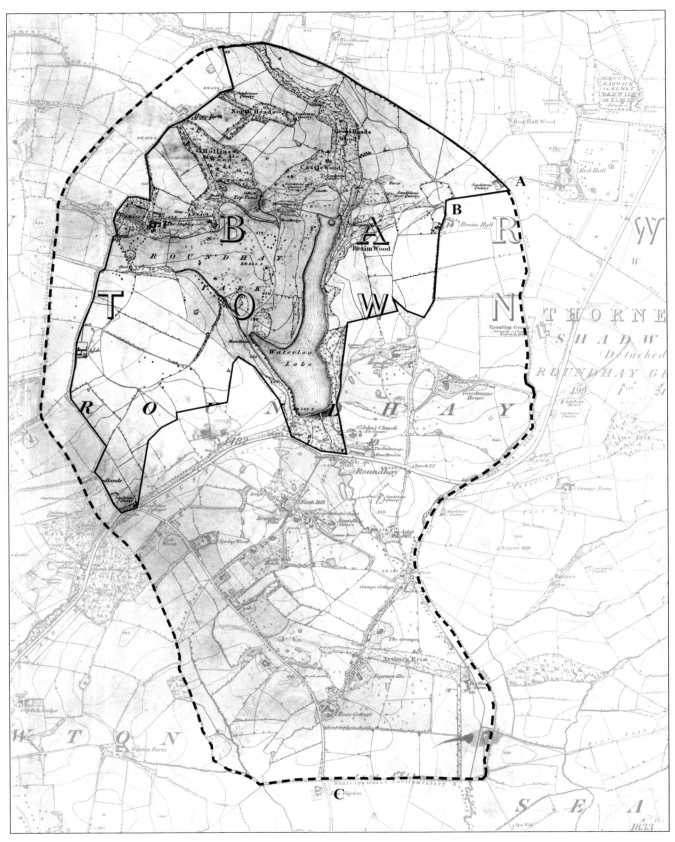

The original bounds of the hunting park can be clearly delineated on the 6" to the mile OS map published in 1850. The main medieval entrance (A) led directly to the hunting lodge (B). The southern gate (C) gave easy access to the ore fields. The solid line delineates the approximate bounds of the park today.

R oundhay Park lies only three miles to the north of Leeds, yet it remained outside the bounds of the city until 1912. The survival of this great medieval hunting park and its transformation into one of the finest municipal parks in the country is a most fortunate and remarkable accident of history. The baron's hunting park was remodelled by a wealthy banker as a desirable country estate. Then an acrimonious family dispute resulted in its sale to a visionary Victorian businessman, who even mortgaged his own home to obtain it for the people of Leeds! The history of the park is a fascinating story of power, prestige and self-interest which has produced Leeds' greatest jewel.

The Round Hay

Roundhay Park is well over nine hundred years old and derives its name from the circular 'hay' or 'round enclosure' created at the end of the eleventh century as a hunting park for members of the Norman aristocracy. Hunting was one of the favourite activities of the nobility and during the medieval period around two thousand of these enclosures were constructed, including Leeds Park and Rothwell Hay.[1] Deer were held of the King and hunting rights were a jealously guarded privilege granted only to favoured members of the court. A deer park contained three essential elements - a tract of wild, semi-wooded land enclosed by a ditch, earth bank, hedge or fence; accommodation for the hunters, park officials, horses and dogs; and finally the deer. They were contained within the confines of the park and kept under control for breeding.[2]

Though Roundhay is not mentioned in the Domesday Book of 1086, the enclosed area formed part of the estates granted to Ilbert de Lacy by William the Conqueror. Ilbert was a powerful Norman baron who received extensive lands in return for the loyal support he had given the King throughout his military campaigns, particularly the brutal crushing of the Anglo-Scandinavian revolt of 1069, known as the 'harrying of the North'. The first mention of 'Lerundeheia' is in a charter of 1153, whereby Henry de Lacy confirmed the grant of 'those lands next to the Roundhay' to the monks of Kirkstall Abbey.[3]

It seems likely that members of the de Lacy family were responsible for creating the original hunting enclosure. This was an enormous undertaking. A vast army of labourers was needed to construct the perimeter bank and ditch, which stretched for almost six miles. Part of the original boundary ditch still survives on the north eastern corner of the estate, and even today this is twenty feet wide by ten feet deep.[4] If the ditch surrounded the whole enclosure it would have involved the removal of around a quarter of a million tons of earth. The 'round hay' was then fenced with vertical pales of oak. A circular shape was chosen as it offered the maximum area of enclosed land for the minimum amount of fencing. The original bounds of the park can clearly be seen on the 1850 Ordnance Survey Map opposite. It is possible to identify the location of the medieval park gates which were constructed at critical access points around the perimeter.

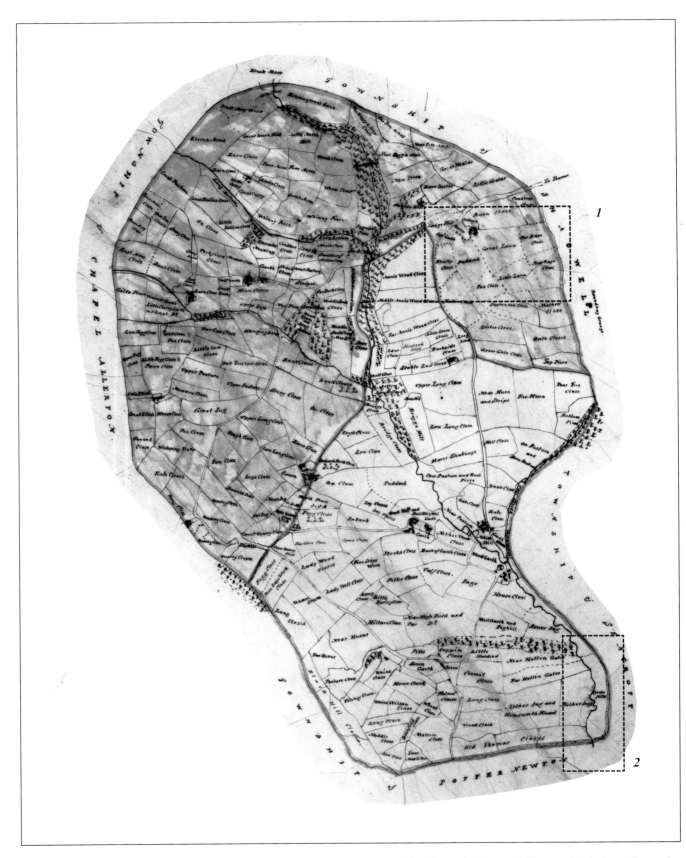

A plan of the Township of Roundhay drawn by Jonathan Taylor in 1803 for Samuel Elam and Thomas Nicholson. Samuel held the land to the south. Note how the former hunting park is by this time virtually denuded of trees. Area 1 shows the location of the hunting lodge and 2 an iron working site.

This boundary fence needed constant maintenance. The first documentary evidence we have of this is 'The Account of Robert de Halton, reeve' for 1373-4, which notes:

And in agreement made with divers men planting boards, posts and rails, made of six oaks felled by the purchasers of the bark, and with the same making sixty eight acres of paling between Allerton Gate and Scholes Carr, and between Gipton Hirne and Seacroft Wood, by order of the chief forester, reckoning at 12d per acre, 68s.

And one cart hired to carry the said posts, boards and rails from the places where they were felled to the places now newly constructed with the help of the old boards.[5]

Gate pivots are mentioned in the 1420-1 accounts, when 4d was spent on the purchase of two gudgeons and plates 'bought for the gates of the park'.[6]

Once the bounds were clearly defined and the wild animals trapped within, the parker and his staff went to enormous lengths to preserve stocks. This was no easy task, particularly in the winter when food was scarce. Losses could be substantial in the winter months and diseases called the garget and the rotte flourished in confined herds.[7] An interesting insight into the annual cycle of work can be gained from the accounts of 1373-4:

And in the wages of five men cutting brushwood and other trees for feeding the deer in the winter season of this year, viz, each of them at different times for forty days, at 2d per day.

And in six cartloads of hay to support the deer in the ensuing winter, in a place called le Stannk - 20s.

And in the hire of one cart to carry the hay from le Stannk to the Grange within the park by six turns at 8d a turn.

And in wages of one man driving the said cart and helping to stow the said hay in the Grange, for four days, taking by the day 3d - 12d for this year.[8]

The lord would contact the parker to arrange a suitable time for the hunt. He would travel to Roundhay accompanied by a huge retinue of friends and servants. The hunting lodge provided basic accommodation for members of the party, along with their horses and dogs. Very little is known about this important medieval building. It was almost certainly located on the site of Cobble Hall Farm. 'Lodge Hill' is clearly marked on Jonathan Taylor's plan of 1803.[9] Furthermore we know that it was located 'within the lawn of the park' and that the two adjoining fields to Cobble Hall Farm are called 'Great Lawn' and 'Little Lawn'.

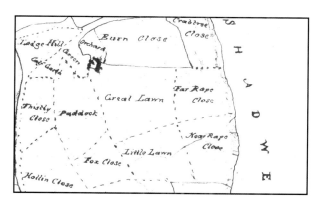

Extract 1 from Jonathan Taylor's Plan of 1803 (opposite) showing the site of the medieval hunting lodge at the top of Lodge Hill.

This is significant as the designers of the park deliberately created these areas of lush grass near the hunting lodge to encourage the deer to graze there.

Fair Benefield whose care to thee doth surely cleave
Which bears a grass as soft as is the dainty silk
And so thick and deep that the proud palmed deer
Forsake the closer woods and make their quiet leir
In beds of platted fog (thick grass)[10]

Medieval beaters drove the deer out of the forest on to 'the lawn' so that the less vigorous hunters, who did not wish to take part in the chase, could simply step out of the lodge and use bow and arrows to shoot the deer gathered in front of them!

The hunt was an elaborate affair with its own rules and customs. If it was the chase, a particular deer would be singled out from the herd.

The chief huntsman, noting its exact position, would lead the hounds to that precise spot in order for the dogs to pick up the scent. Thereafter the hounds would only pursue that deer. The hunters followed behind, until the quarry was dragged down by the pack and killed. At other times deer were chased into narrow valleys, like The Gorge, where archers were waiting to shoot them. Once the kill had been made the huntsmen were rewarded with a complicated distribution of hides and venison. The offal or 'humbles' were given to the lowliest servants, hence the expression 'to eat humble pie'.

In the early medieval period hunters used spears, knives and bows to kill the deer. Fine horses were specially bred for the hunt. Mastiffs and a large breed of greyhound were much prized, yet costly to keep. William Wheater, the Victorian historian, states that in September 1212 King John visited the 'Roundhay' and spent three days hunting in the park with a pack of over two hundred hounds. He claimed that the cost of the hounds alone was 58s 4fid, over half a year's wage for a skilled roofer![11]

The Lodge, like the fencing around the park, needed constant maintenance. Robert de Halton's Accounts indicate that by 1373 it was in need of major roof repairs:

And in two cartloads of thackstone* (stone slates) bought at Shadwell for the repairing the roof of the lodge within the lawn of the park, with 8d given for the carriage of the same to the said lodge - 2s.

And in wages to three tilers roofing the said lodge, for two days at 5d a day each - 2s 6d.

And for 200 nails bought for the laths under the said slates, to be fixed in the roof aforesaid - 6s.

And in wages of one woman gathering moss for the said slates to be laid upon, for one day - 2d.[12]

Sixty years later the Lodge was once again 'ruinous'.[13] By this time the deer population appears to have been in decline and on the 21st February 1503, Sir Thomas Wortley, the King's Steward, could only 'view' thirty four beasts. Its days as a hunting park were numbered.[14]

Although its prime function was that of a hunting park, this large tract of enclosed land provided other forms of income for the holder of the estate. The natural riches of the park were exploited to the full by medieval landlords.

Timber

Throughout the medieval period wood remained the chief form of building material and source of fuel. It was a carefully guarded asset, yet the landlord was dependent on the honesty and diligence of the forester and his men to ensure that wood was not removed from the park without due authority. Coppicing and pollarding ensured that the woods remained productive for long periods and even the bark was harvested for use in the tanning process.

Surviving accounts show that timber was regularly sent for the repair of manorial buildings in Leeds. Initially wood for the town had been supplied from 'Leeds Park', a medieval enclosure that stretched westwards from Park Row towards what is today the Yorkshire Post building on Wellington Street.[15] This woodland was quickly depleted and landowners had to go farther afield for their timber. In 1399 fifty eight shillings was paid for the wages of nine carpenters involved in cutting timber at Roundhay, Seacroft and Rothwell for the repair of Leeds Dam, swept away in 'the great flood'.[16] This dam held back the waters of the River Aire and diverted them to the waterwheels at the King's Mill, Swinegate, the main corn grinding mill of the district and a monopoly that provided a useful form of income for the Lord of the Manor. Another manorial monopoly was the common oven, located off Kirkgate, where the townsfolk had to bake their bread. This also became dependent on wood from the 'Round Hay'

and in 1507 over 1800 faggots were carted to the town to be burnt in the common oven.[17] Thus the park became a vital source of timber and fuel for the burgeoning town of Leeds.

Rights of grazing and pasturage

In 1152, Henry de Lacy helped Abbot Alexander and a small number of Cistercian monks from Barnoldswick, to establish a monastery at Kirkstall.[18] The family were generous benefactors and in addition to the site at Kirkstall bestowed certain lands upon them, including around two hundred acres of land at Roundhay, just to the east of the enclosed hunting park. Here they constructed a substantial farmhouse with extensive outbuildings, later called Roundhay Grange.

Roundhay Grange and location as shown on the 1850 OS Map

Around 1200 Roger de Lacy, provided the abbot with a new charter that not only confirmed his family's gift of land at Roundhay, but also reaffirmed the monks' valuable grazing rights within the park for 'forty cows with their bull calves and their sheep they have customarily held there, plus forty swine at the acorn time'.[19] In addition he instructed his forester to provide them with two oak trees a year for the repair of their farm buildings.

Iron ore workings and coal extraction

In medieval times an extensive iron ore and coal field lay beneath Seacroft and the southern half of Roundhay. After the Norman Conquest the pioneers in iron production were the monks of Kirkstall, who followed the example of their French brothers and organised the mining and smelting of metals on a large scale.[20] This was a lucrative business which brought rich rewards to the monks.

In 1160 William de Somerville, one of the de Lacy's tenants, granted them the right to operate iron bloomeries at Seacroft and Roundhay on condition that the abbey provided iron for his ploughs.[21] This important grant was made a mere eight years after the monks had established themselves at Kirkstall.

Two essential elements were required for the production of iron - iron ore and charcoal.

The monks knew the location of the ore and the 'round hay' and woodlands of Seacroft provided raw material for the charcoal burners.

Iron making involved an army of skilled craftsmen including miners, charcoal burners, smiths and other ancilliary staff. The nature of the grant allowed these workers into restricted areas of the hunting park - a privilege not extended to the ordinary tenants.[22]

The ore was dug using bell-pits, whose diameters increased as they became deeper. The point at which the excavation became dangerous, due to potential collapse, determined when it would be abandoned. Further pits were then dug, following the seam.

In his grant, William allowed miners to dig bell-pits but insisted that these hazardous holes were back-filled once the ore had been extracted. The ore was then washed to remove clay and other surface debris, before being crushed into smaller pieces. This process was performed by hand or water powered stamps. Tradition has it that women and even children undertook this work. The ore was then roasted to remove sulphur and water.

Meanwhile the charcoal burners had been busy cutting and collecting wood, which they chopped into short logs. These were piled systematically into heaps in the form of a 'flattened beehive', about the height of a man, which were then covered over with freshly cut turves to exclude air from the wood being carbonised. A small hole was left in the crown of the dome to permit the emission of fumes.

Once complete a fire was started within and the wood was allowed to burn slowly until the product was charcoal.

At the furnace site workers built a hearth of sandstone and surrounded it with low circular walls of the same rough rock. Cleaned ore was placed at one side; the charcoal at the other. When the charcoal had been lit, air was blown in to produce the hot gas which passed into the ore to release the metallic iron.

Air was added via a tube attached to foot or water powered bellows. Charcoal was continually added until the 'ore-blower' sensed that the 'blow' was complete. Temperatures of 1000 - 1200 degrees celsius could be achieved.

Charcoal burning. The coppiced wood is cut (A) and transported in cut lengths(B). It is then stacked (C) and the turf cut (D). The turf is used to cover the stack (E) and the wood is ignited through a small hole in the base. The fumes escape into the air. The stack is allowed to cool for two weeks before being dismantled (F). At this point the charcoal is thrown through a sieve (G) and the large pieces are then used in the furnace. The smaller pieces are used for heating the cooking pots. The charcoal burner's family live on site and participate in the work.

This process produced a mass of slag together with pieces of iron intermingled with cinders. After it had cooled and become relatively brittle, it was smashed using large hammers. This separated the small pieces of spongy iron from the cinders.

Where the workings were extensive, as in Roundhay, this led to sizeable mounds of waste slag and in the south eastern corner of the park a long, slender tongue of land abutting Wyke Beck, became known as 'Cynder Hills'.[23]

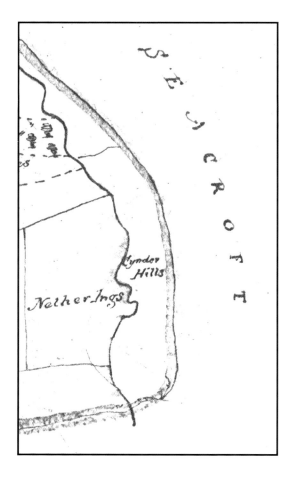

Enlargement 2 from Jonathan Taylor's Plan of 1803 showing the location of 'Cynder Hills'.

The small lumps of iron were transferred to the finery where they were reheated and struck on the anvil to create an ingot, at the same time squeezing out any remaining slag. This process produced pure iron. Since this quality was attained by hammering, it became known as 'wrought' iron.

The metal was finally taken to a forge, where the blacksmith reheated the iron before hammering or chiseling it into a variety of shapes, including horse shoes, waggon tyres, metal tools and cooking utensils.

For over a century the monks of Kirkstall exploited the natural resources here. None of the operators would have been monks but the Cistercians used the iron product solely to generate cash. Despite such income, successive abbots proved to be too pious - poor financial managers who allowed the abbey to teeter on the edge of bankruptcy. In 1276 the situation was compounded by a devastating outbreak of disease among their sheep. Their plight was desperate and debts amounted to £5248![24] In 1280 Abbot Gilbert de Cotles was forced to resign and the following year the monks applied for permission to disperse. Instead Hugh de Grimston, a local man, was appointed abbot. He valiantly tried to stave off bankruptcy and brokered a complex financial agreement with the de Lacy family. Hugh was allowed to draw money from the family's account in return for certain lands, including Roundhay. Monkish iron making ceased but by the end of Hugh's term of office the debt had been reduced to a mere £160, nevertheless, the loss of Roundhay and Seacroft was a bitter blow.[25]

It was the de Lacy family who now controlled the mineral rights. Just like the Cistercians, the new owners soon began to exploit the iron ore fields. The first known record of a smelting furnace at Roundhay is found in accounts of 1295-6, when the 'issue' for seven weeks work amounted to £3 3s 0d.[26] 1322 proved to be a particularly busy year for the miners and iron workers who spent an exhausting twenty two weeks producing iron.

At Roundhay Forge the smiths laboured for nineteen weeks, hammering the metal into a myriad of different shapes. They almost certainly provided the ironwork for the waterwheels and machinery at Leeds corn mill. The income from the forge alone was £8 18s 4d - an enormous sum of money! It seems likely that they employed water driven bellows to speed up production.[27]

Medieval iron production involved a whole range of a dirty, smoky, destructive processes that marred vast swathes of land in the southern half of the hunting park - destroying tree cover, leaving ugly mounds of waste as well as frightening the wildlife. Land owners were reluctant to agree to such destruction. The lord had to constantly balance the financial benefits gained by allowing iron production to take place, against the impact on the deer park. The detrimental effect on the lord's estate is reflected in the Reeve's Accounts for 1491-2 when the farmer was given an allowance of 13s 4d 'because the grass there is destroyed and occupied by the working of an iron mine this year.'[28] However, as tree cover was removed, a critical factor became the supply of wood to make charcoal. This is made very clear in the Rental for 1424-5 which states 'there is there a certain iron mine which is worth nothing yearly unless there has been a sale of dry underwood, and if there has the mine is worth 12d weekly and the dead wood for burning weekly 19s.'[29] However the supplies of ironstone were also becoming exhausted and by the sixteenth century production had ceased completely.

Iron ore was not the only natural resource extracted from beneath the ground of Roundhay. Marl pits were dug for manure, clay extracted for pottery production and the rich band of coal was constantly exploited by medieval miners. So deep did the workings become that water driven pumps had to be used to extract the water.[30] Like the iron workings, these activities scarred the landscape. Even the beautiful beck that ran through the park was altered. In 1577 Elizabeth I granted Christopher Mather permission to dam Wyke Beck at Ellers Close, a small clearing just inside the park. He constructed a leat from there to his new watermill at Seacroft and regularly brought his carts and drays into the park to service the dam and his water courses.[31] By 1628 the supplies of coal were exhausted and the survey noted that the tenure of the 'mines of coal in Roundhay and Roundhay Grange late in the tenure of John Carpenter' had been worth 6s 8d but are now 'out of use'.[32]

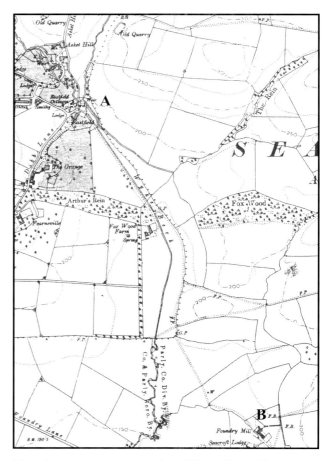

Map showing watercourse from Ellers Close (A) to Foundry Mill (B).

Deforestation and the end of the hunting park

By the 15th century the park formed part of the royal estates. On 5th March 1486 King Henry VII granted a seven year lease to William Nettleton of certain lands in Roundhay, Shadwell, Leeds and Thorner. Under the agreement William had to 'keep all the premises in repair at his own cost, taking timber and thackstone from the park of Roundhay and the woods of Seacroft, at Shadwell and at le Stone Delph there.'[33] Nettleton clearly abused his power and systematically stripped the park of large quantities of mature timber. This process continued until 1503 when Sir John Neville, the new keeper of the park, complained to the King. Sir Thomas Wortley was sent to investigate and was horrified to find that vast amounts of timber had indeed been felled and removed from the park, including at least twenty six oak trees, which had not been 'marked for the King's use with the King's axe'. Sir Thomas stressed that this was just a simple estimate as 'no man knows the whole number of the waste and destruction for the ground where they grew is overgrown with bushes.'[34] Furthermore Nettleton was accused of taking wood to prop up his windmill.

He vehemently denied the charges, claiming that he had only removed his just entitlement. Wortley's investigations, however, revealed that hundreds of waggon loads of timber had been removed from the park and that key families of the district were implicated in the trade. Ironically, twenty three years later a commission found Sir John Neville guilty of 'wastage of timber' in Roundhay Park! [35]

The reduction of tree cover constantly diminished the habitat so vital for the survival of the deer. The last indication of there being any left in the park is a grant of free warren made on 6th June 1599 by which John Darcy, knight, was allowed to kill 'all Fallow Deer, Wild Beasts, Stags and Conies'.[36] Yet the process of deforestation continued apace and future lessees of the park were to be equally ruthless.

When Charles I came to the throne in 1625 part of his inheritance was Roundhay. Desperately short of money, he borrowed heavily from the Corporation of London.[37] In 1628, in order to settle his debts and raise more funds, he gave many estates, including Roundhay to the Corporation. Naturally they sent surveyors to establish the value of this property. They noted that Hall Wood 'hath now no wood in it but a few shrubs and old trees' and that the land was now being used for pasture. Stephen Tempest leased a large part of the estate, much of which had recently been denuded of trees. When they visited Wood Hall Carr, an area of some fifty eight acres, the surveyors were alarmed to discover that 'the wood hath been lately much spoiled and wasted by ye present tenant Mr Stephen Tempest'. They clearly had a sense of humour, noting 'we found so many good trees down and stacked up by the roots and some barked though yet standing we could not but imagine there had been a tempest in them.' They tried to gather evidence against Tempest, but he was clearly a brutish individual and the surveyors noted that many of the copyholders were 'fearful to speak the truth.' [38]

The removal of trees was directly accompanied by an increase in agricultural activity within the bounds of the park. New farms were established with the cleared land being used for arable and pastoral farming. Fields were enclosed and given specific names. The change in the game available for the hunter is well illustrated by contrasting the grant to John Darcy, which included fallow deer and stags, to that of a later owner of the park, Lord Stourton, who in 1779 was allowed 'to kill all such hares, partridges, pheasants and other game.'[39] The deer had gone forever and the hunting rights were no longer regarded as the park's most important asset. In 1797 the 1,300 acre estate, virtually denuded of tree cover, peppered with less than a dozen farmhouses and subdivided into relatively unproductive fields, was placed on the market by Charles Philip, the 17th Baron of Stourton .[40] No single purchaser was forthcoming, however, on 4th August 1803, the estate was eventually purchased by two Leeds born Quakers, Samuel Elam and Thomas Nicholson, for the princely sum of £58,000.[41]

Once the property had been purchased, Elam and Nicholson employed Jonathan Taylor, a Leeds surveyor, to draw a detailed plan of the estate (Page 4).[42] This delineated the extent of each partner's land - Samuel held the land to the south, which he intended to develop for housing, while Thomas decided to create a country estate with a magnificent mansion house. The dotted line makes clear the dividing line. Note how the former hunting park is by this time virtually denuded of trees and is divided up into small parcels of agricultural land.

Roundhay was an isolated place and could only be reached along centuries old cart tracks. In 1802 there had been talk of a turnpike from Leeds and this may have influenced their decision to buy.

Samuel Elam, was born in 1773.[43] His father died when he was three years old and he spent much of his early childhood at the Friends Boarding School, Gildersome. On attaining his majority he inherited the bulk of his father's fortune. He clearly had a flair for business and swiftly became engaged in a wide range of activities, including the export of locally produced cloth to America.[44] By 1803 he was a partner in the banking firm of Thompson, Elam and Holtby, with branches in Leeds and Bridlington.[45] Elam clearly viewed the purchase of his Roundhay estate as yet another speculative venture and instantly sold off parcels of land to his first cousin, Robert Elam.[46]

Some of Samuel's other investments were unsound and the five year delay in developing the turnpike from Leeds must have deterred potential buyers. By 1810 he was in dire financial straits having clearly over-stretched himself. Once again he employed Jonathan Taylor to produce a detailed plan of his estate and in October of that year advertised over four hundred acres for sale.[47] On the same day as the advertisement appeared in the local press, his partners, Thompson and Holtby, announced that they would continue in business without him. Eight weeks later Elam was bankrupt and all claimants were asked to submit statements so that the estate might be 'put into a train of liquidation.'[48] Samuel died on 28th March 1811 at the early age of 37, almost certainly as a result of the stresses and strains brought on by his financial difficulties.

His land was subdivided and various parcels were purchased by Thomas Nicholson and Robert Elam. Samuel's friend and executor, John Goodman, also bought some of the land, but he did not have an easy task as nearly five years passed before Lot 1 was eventually sold to Benjamin Goodman of Hunslet Lane.[49] The completion of the new road to Leeds in 1810 certainly helped to end Roundhay's isolation and former empty plots at long last became filled with elegant stone mansions, complete with lodges, stables and extensive grounds. Just over a decade later it was described as being *'chiefly in the possession of families of opulence connected with the town of Leeds'.* [50] It had become one of the favoured havens of the middle class, away from the smoke, noise and noxious trades of Leeds but most importantly of all, far away from the 'lower orders'. Samuel Elam had seen the potential for such residential development at Roundhay, unfortunately he had mis-timed the purchase.

Unlike Elam, Thomas Nicholson intended from the start to develop his half of the park as a country estate. He was born at Chapel Allerton in 1765. His father, William, was an Anglican clothier of relatively modest means, while his mother, Hannah, was of Quaker stock. It is unclear how Thomas became so fabulously wealthy. In 1786 he was residing in the parish of St.Helen's, Bishopgate, in London and in the same year married Elizabeth Jackson, daughter of a London leather factor. He settled in London and from 1788 to 1806 is listed as an 'Insurance Broker' He was soon living at Artillery Place, Finsbury Square, one of the most fashionable locations in the capital, and in 1806 went into partnership with his half brother, Stephen.[51] About 1813 he founded the bank of Nicholson, Jansen and Co. and continued to prosper, despite the difficult trading conditions created by the Napoleonic Wars. Despite the obvious business advantages of being located in the capital, he never lost sight of his roots and on 22 August 1799, at the age of thirty four, purchased the Chapel Allerton Hall Estate.[52]

He viewed this as an investment and quickly re-let the Hall and its associated properties, only retaining one of the smaller houses for his own use. Four years later he acquired the Roundhay property and thus became one of the largest landowners in the north of Leeds.

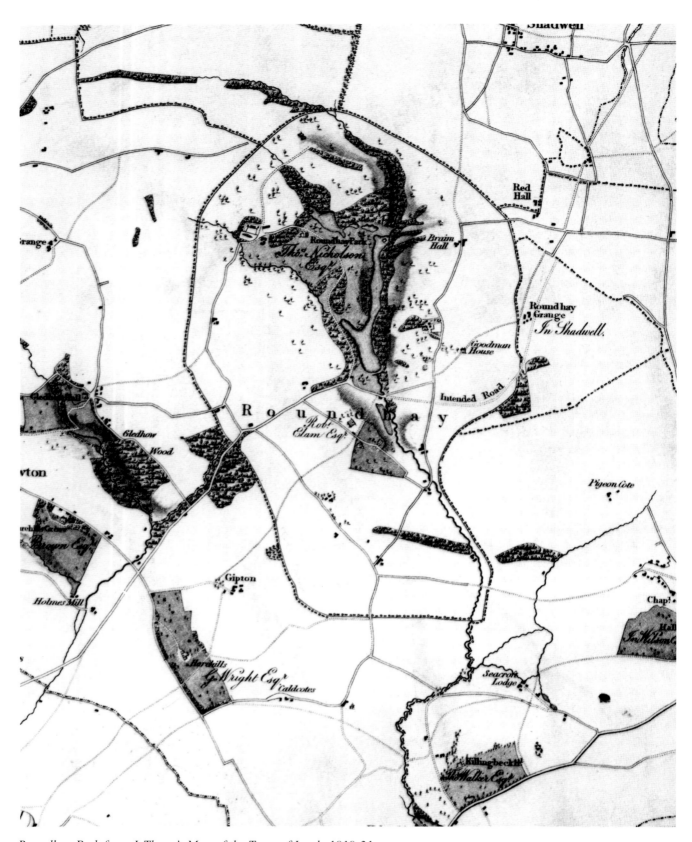

Roundhay Park from J. Thorp's Map of the Town of Leeds 1819-21

This is the first known plan that shows the landscape after Thomas Nicholson's alterations. The Mansion House, Canal Gardens, Top Pond, Castle, and Waterloo Lake are all clearly discernable.

Thomas aspired to the lifestyle of a landed country gentleman. By 1803 the attractions of London had worn thin and he decided to return to Roundhay to be near his family. His half of the estate comprised a number of farms, a patchwork of enclosed fields, three streams and a beautiful tree-lined gorge. With professional assistance, he began the slow process of utilising the existing natural features to create a country estate with landscaped grounds, complete with lakes, ponds and follies. The crowning glory was to be an elegant mansion house.

Careful comparison of the 1803 plan (Page 4) and the Ordnance Survey map of 1850 (Page 2) reveals that workmen had to remove numerous hedgerows, walls and pockets of woodland, before work could start on the construction of the new pleasure grounds. Every aspect was carefully planned so that large open areas of grassland, interspersed with pockets of specially planted woodland, would create wonderful vistas across the park. Winding paths passed in and out of these copses providing magnificent viewpoints and 'controlled scenes of wilderness'.

In the fields to the east of the mansion, clay was used to make an impervious lining for the Top Pond or Upper Lake. Located opposite the main entrance to the house it was constantly fed by a stream of crystal clear water, flowing into the estate through Great Pasture and Eleven Acres. At the eastern end of the lake were dramatic waterfalls and several pools, which were crossed by a single arched rustic bridge. The Top Pond would have been the main lake, but for the fortunate acquisition of a tongue of former Elam land in August 1815, which gave Nicholson ownership of the only part of Great Heads Beck not in his possession.[53] This enabled him to construct the most spectacular feature of the park - Waterloo Lake.

The valley bottom was deepened and widened by workmen before work could start on the construction of the main dam. Trade Directories repeatedly state that this was undertaken by unemployed soldiers who had just returned from the Napoleonic Wars. They claim that it took two years to construct and cost around £15,000.[54]

John Wilson Carmichael's atmospheric view of Waterloo Lake painted in 1838.

The beauties of the Nicholson estate, including the Canal Gardens, Hermitage, Castle and spectacular waterfall were skilfully recorded by the artist working for 'The Graphic' in 1872.

Named after the famous British victory at Waterloo, the lake covered thirty three acres, with an average depth of around sixty feet. Originally called the Waterloo Fish Pond, it had at its southern end a spectacular sixty foot waterfall, created by the sheer wall of the dam. Beneath, the waters ran through a copse, the view being enhanced by the ripple of small falls between the shallow pools.

No fashionable park would have been complete without its follies - 'The Hermitage', like the sham 'Old Castle', provided places of retreat and contemplation. The Hermitage was a summerhouse located near the Upper Lake. Built externally of rough hewn boulders and lined with small hazel sticks arranged in fanciful designs, it had windows on each side of the doorway, filled with plain glass and edged with a stained glass border. Beneath was an arch which served as a boat shelter.

At the head of Waterloo Lake was the Old Castle. Built in 1821 by George Nettleton, master builder, it served as another summerhouse. The last footman of the Nicholsons, Charles Mills, recalled that:

Pheasants were bred in Castle Field and Keeper's Garth and luncheon was served in the Old Castle when shooting parties were out. In those days there was a wooden roof on the Old Castle and it had an upper room in which the Nicholson girls did their sewing. They would have tea served there, and from the windows they had as lovely a view as can be imagined.[55]

To the west of the Mansion the tiny stream running through Rush Close was used to feed a large, rectangular, stone-lined pond. This became the central feature of the self contained 'Canal Garden' complete with rustic bridges and arbour.

It was enclosed with brick walls and edged with bedding. The separation of the flower garden from the house was all in vogue, and in line with the thinking of Joshua Major of Leeds (c1787 - 1866) who, in his popular book 'The Theory and Practice of Landscape Gardening' argued that:

The flower garden ought never to be visible from the windows as the appearance of numerous beds and walks, by interrupting the repose and extent of the lawn, has a tendency to destroy its boldness and importance...and the practice of huddling all the most interesting objects possible into one scene is a decided mistake.[56]

THE MANSION — ROUNDHAY PARK.
SOUTH AND WEST FRONTS

There were hothouses and assorted glasshouses in the walled kitchen garden, which lay immediately north of the Canal Garden. This whole area was approached from the great house, along a newly constructed carriage way. But what of the Mansion itself?

The Mansion

Thomas Nicholson required a country house that was not ruinously expensive to build and maintain, yet mirrored the taste of the county elite. The Mansion, in the latest Greek Revival style, was the perfect accommodation for a successful businessman. Occupying an elevated position near the centre of the estate, with superb views over the park, it epitomized good taste of the period and provided an elegant focal point to the estate.

Visitors gained access to the house by passing through the gates at the two entrance lodges (above)

adjoining the Leeds and Wetherby Road, before travelling for three quarters of a mile along the carriage drive, with 'a scene of unusual beauty' on each side.[57]

This classical building, built in ashlar on two storeys with seven bays and an impressive Ionic portico, is almost certainly the work of Thomas Taylor, one of the first professional architects to live in Leeds. Thomas Nicholson's desire to move north is reflected in the fact that on 1st March 1813, in partnership with his half brother Stephen, William Williams Brown and Timothy Rhodes, he opened the Union Bank in Commercial Street, Leeds.[58] The partners were delighted that the new building had been completed in such a rapid time and were clearly impressed by the efficient way Thomas Taylor had undertaken his commission.[59] He was later responsible for St. John's Church, Roundhay, another Nicholson building.

Quite when Thomas and his wife, Elizabeth, moved into the Mansion is unclear. It seems likely that he used his small house at Chapel Allerton as the base from which he supervised the building work. It must have been an enormous relief to finally take possession of such a magnificent house. Quaker records show that he and his wife had moved to Roundhay by 1819.[60]

His new home had numerous stylish rooms and the 1871 sale details give some feel for their size and number:

It contains on the ground floor a handsome vestibule 22'2" by 11'10", a central hall 27' by 25', from the middle of which rises a broad double flight of stairs, lighted from the roof; a library 27'6" by 19'9"; a dining room 27'6" by 18'9", a drawing room 33' by 22'10", a study 16' square and a morning room 22'6" by 16'6". The principal rooms on the ground floor are 13' high and fitted with handsome Marble Mantel-pieces and mahogany framed plate glass windows.[61]

On the first floor were seventeen bedrooms with two up-to-date water closets. Downstairs there was a kitchen, scullery, three larders, storerooms and butler's pantry; while in the basement a laundry and extensive wine cellars.

Thomas died on 14th January 1821, having spent over fifteen years landscaping the grounds and building the Mansion - a home he had lived in for such a short time! Two months later Thomas Hampshire, from a valuation company based on Trinity Lane, Leeds, arrived to make a full inventory of the contents of his house. The fifty nine page booklet lists and values virtually every item and provides a wonderful insight into the sumptuous fixtures and fittings to be found in each room of the Mansion.

He began in the Dining Room:

	£	s	d
Fender and Fix Irons	3	-	-
Turkey Floor Carpet	24	-	-
Hearth Rug	1	10	-
Branch Candlestick	0	10	-
6 Chimney Ornaments	1	-	-
2 Bell Pulls	1	-	-
Sliding Fire Screen	3	-	-
Mahogany Side Board	20	-	-
2 Bronze Pedestals with			
* Patent Lamps*	10	-	-
2 Knife Cases	5	5	-
Plate Warmer	1	5	-
Mirror	20	-	-
15 Mahogany Chairs	45	-	-
3 Window Curtains			
* 3 Venetian Blinds, Cornice)*			
* 12 Pins*	15	-	-
2 Dining Tables	20	-	-

The total value of items in that room alone came to £170 10s - enough to build two workers' cottages! Room after room was crammed with valuable furniture, ornaments, carpets and paintings. His silverware was valued at £226 4s 6d, while the contents of his substantial library came to £228 13 s 0d. The total value of the house contents was £2251 - a fortune![62]

In addition there was an elegant stable block (below) at a discreet distance from the house, with a nearby cluster of modern housing for his estate workers.

The Stable Block may well have been the work of the architect John Clarke. The clock was made in 1864 by William Potts of Leeds, though it used the bell of the previous clock, dated 1826.

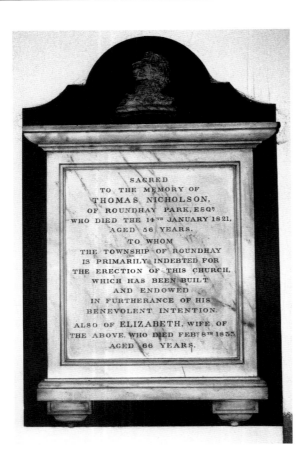

Thomas Nicholson's Legacy

This wonderful mansion and associated landscape were the result of one man's fortune and vision. When he died in 1821, aged just 56, the house and its grounds were almost complete - a lasting memorial to the 'local boy made good'. In less than twenty years Thomas Nicholson had created one of the most outstanding landscapes in the county, which, with its naturalised features of lakes and clumps of trees set sympathetically within the rolling landform of Roundhay, provide a fitting tribute to the picturesque landscape movement. Thomas and his gardeners exercised considerable skill in creating such a stunning landscape from former unproductive agricultural land.

Thomas was interred at Camp Lane Court, the Quaker burial ground in Leeds, leaving his wife, Elizabeth, to reside in the house for a further eleven years.

The Nicholson Family

Thomas had no children and so left the bulk of his fortune, including his Roundhay property, to his half-brother Stephen. The two had been business partners for over fifteen years and it seemed fitting that he should inherit. One of the key features of any private estate was a place of worship. It had long been rumoured that Thomas intended to build a church at Roundhay, and the rector of Barwick, in whose parish Roundhay lay, had responded by promising to assign £200 per annum for a minister.[63]

It was left to Stephen to carry out Thomas's wishes. On 8th April 1824 the Leeds Intelligencer announced that a new Anglican church would be erected at Roundhay at the sole expense of Stephen Nicholson (right). His private bill had just gone through Parliament and, as was customary, the patronage of the church was vested in him and his heirs forever. Once again, Thomas Taylor was appointed architect and on Wednesday 22nd September 1824 the first stone was laid by the Rev. William Hiley Bathurst, rector of Barwick-in-Elmet. A lavish dinner of roast beef and plum pudding was provided for the workmen and their families.[64] A newspaper reporter estimated this to be three to four hundred people! The consecration took place in January 1826, though it was to be another three months before the church finally opened its doors for services.[65]

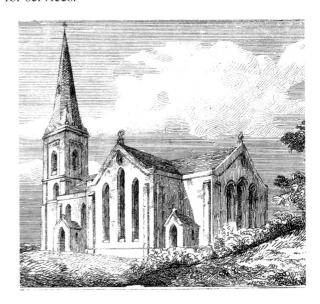

*View of Roundhay in 1849
by W. R. Robinson.*

Stephen's generosity did not end there. In 1833 he arranged for the construction of a row of robust almshouses near the church. These almshouses (above) were for use by old servants of the Nicholson family or 'persons residing in the townships of Roundhay, Shadwell, Chapel Allerton or Potternewton but with preference for the first class'. There was a new Day School but 'no child [is] to be admitted whose parents would prevent its attendance at Roundhay Church and the Sunday School'.[66] This was an 'enclosed world' and there is no record of the Nicholsons becoming involved in any of the charitable activities in the nearby town of Leeds.

In December 1801 Stephen married Sarah Rhodes, the daughter of a wealthy Leeds merchant. It is unclear when they moved from London. It is known that he was tenant at Braim (Cobble) Hall, Roundhay, in November 1824 and throughout this period was actively involved in the construction of two other residences, Springwood and Ladywood Farm.

He built a stylish mansion on the site of a former farm and called this property Roundhay Lodge. He engaged Taylor to complete a mansion called North Hill and by 1826 he had made this his home. He had to wait a further seven years for the death of his sister-in-law before he could move into 'The Mansion' itself.

Stephen and Sarah enjoyed living in 'The Great House' pampered by nine house servants who catered for their every whim. However, as in Thomas's case, the union was not blessed with children and, as a result, the nagging question of who should inherit their fortune needed to be addressed. The matter was resolved when, on 13th October 1827, Stephen's nephew, William Nicholson Philips, changed his surname to Nicholson by Royal Licence, and at the age of twenty three became sole heir to the estate.[67] Eleven days earlier he had married Martha Rhodes, third and youngest daughter of Abram Rhodes of Wold Newton Hall, and a close relative of Stephen's wife.

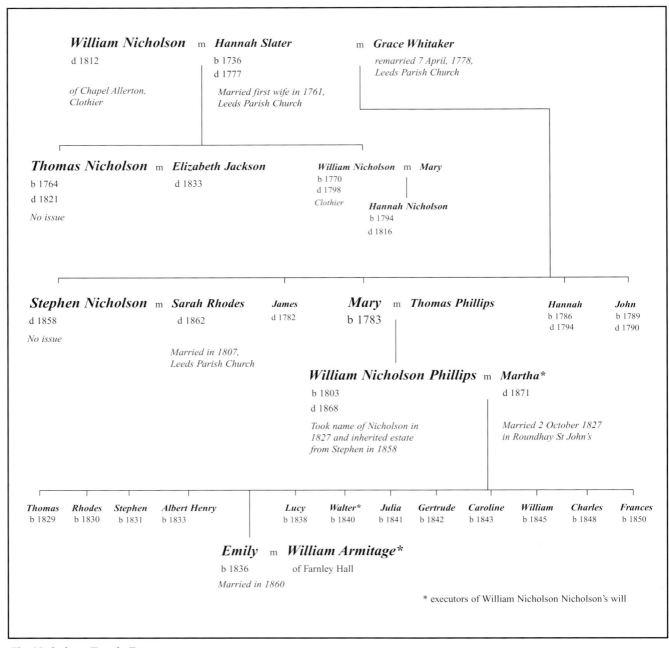

The Nicholson Family Tree.

William had already obtained a masters degree from Cambridge University when he went to live with his wife, Martha, in Heavitree, near Exeter. As Stephen and Sarah became old, William brought his family to live at Park Cottage, a sizable house at Roundhay. Unlike his uncles, William had no difficulty in producing heirs and his wife, Martha, bore him over a dozen children! [68]

Once established at Roundhay the two families enjoyed a close relationship.

In 1906 William's daughter, Emily, wrote her memoirs in which she vividly remembered visiting her aged relatives at 'The Great House' :

They had no children and we were rather in awe of them for they were grand and stiff. Two of us went every day in the middle of the day to dine with our uncle and aunt at the Large House and sometimes used to play a game of chess with our aunt. [69]

Their happiness was to be short lived.

During the first few months of 1840 Stephen became increasingly concerned about the number of burglaries in the district. As a result, he asked staff to keep an armed guard on his premises and those of his nephew, William Nicholson Nicholson. On 18th May, at around one o'clock in the morning, Stephen's gamekeeper, Charles Thompson, took shelter from the rain in the entrance porch to William's house. Unfortunately he nodded off to sleep and his gun hit the door. The family dog barked and woke William's wife, Martha. She heard noises and, assuming it was a house breaker, quickly roused her husband. A burglar had attempted to break in the week before and so William took no chances. He went to get assistance from his groom before undertaking any investigation. They both approached the door with great caution.[70]

The following turn of events were to haunt William for the rest of his life. His groom recalled the tragic accident with great clarity:

We went towards the front door and I saw a man whom I did not know, knelt down as if attempting to prize the door open and prize it loose. My master, who was behind, called out 'Holloa, what do you want there?' The man did not speak, and master immediately fired at him, and he rushed forward, and the man levelled his gun at me. My master fired the second barrel in my defence, when the deceased attempted to shoot me.[71]

As he lay dying, the poor gamekeeper made a sworn statement in which he exonerated William Nicholson Nicholson of all blame. He claimed that he hadn't recognised the two men and that it had been his intention to shoot them both, as he assumed that they were the housebreakers. Charles was well armed. One barrel of his gun was loaded with No.4 shot and the other with six pistol bullets. He also had a loaded revolver with him.

The family surgeon, Mr Cass, was immediately summoned and remained with the wounded gamekeeper for over four hours. He could do little as the injuries were so severe. Some cordials were given and a poultice applied to the wound.

He tried bleeding him and even applied leeches, but by five o'clock Thompson was dead.

The coroner returned a verdict of death by misadventure. The Rev. Armitage Rhodes remarked

'I, think, gentlemen, that this inquiry will serve to show to all of us the necessity of the most extreme caution in the use of firearms.'[72]

When Charles Thompson realised he was dying he expressed concern for his wife and children. William stressed that he should not *'distress his mind, as they should never want.'* The deceased man left a wife and four children - the eldest being twelve - the youngest four. He is buried in St. John's churchyard beneath an inscribed stone which reads:

In Memory of Charles George Thompson
Game Keeper of Roundhay Park
Who Died May 19th 1840
Aged 49 years

Brief time death's cruel summons gave
Between his duty and the grave
He roams no more the woodland round
Nor hears the Guns deep starting sound
While friends and kindred o'er him weep
He calmly takes this last cold sleep

Family Life

The accident had a profound effect on William Nicholson Nicholson. Locals maintained that he never ' looked up' after the incident and his daughter, Emily recalled that while her mother was always cheerful, her father remained 'very grave'.[73]

Life for his children became dull and regimented. The family's diet was spartan. Although they ate meat and pudding at lunch, the rest of the meals in summer consisted of large basins of milk with cream and dry bread, though in winter he generously allowed the milk to be warmed! They were given a piece of dry bread and butter in the morning with a further slice at supper time. This was a deeply religious family and Bible reading took place every morning before breakfast. Other reading was strictly limited to Christian texts including ' biography of god's people in olden times'.

Emily remembered her childhood with little affection:

My life did not have many remarkable things in it; it all seemed to go on in a regular routine, new brothers and sisters arriving, the old nurse continually holding up her finger and shushing me for fear I would wake the baby.

Though my life was rather hard and monotonous yet I thank the lord very much for it. There was a nice governess and I was glad of her companionship, I helped to teach the children all the morning and in the afternoon went with my mother if she went shopping or calling. Sometimes I read in the woods where I had wonderful times.[74]

One of the highlights of her life was visiting St. John's on a Sunday. She travelled there in her uncle's 'grand yellow chariot' with two footmen with white stockings standing behind. After the morning service they returned to the Mansion for dinner, before returning for the three o'clock service. Her favourite time was what the children called 'Weeping Sundays'.

Certain Sundays in the year were very much marked because Mr Rhodes, a retired clergyman, used to weep as he read the lessons and we always looked forward to those. The Sundays about Esau and Jacob and the Sunday about Joseph in the pit were always weeping Sundays and Mrs Rhodes, in her pew, wept too. The Vicar, Mr Davis, was quite in advance of his time and preached things not considered quite orthodox. When he did so Mr Armitage Rhodes coughed and we all listened with eager ears to the heresy being propounded.[75]

The Nicholson family had the usual worries about their children and they were fortunate that Stephen took such an interest in his great nieces and nephews, helping to promote their interests through his network of contacts. In October 1841 we find him writing to the Earl of Harewood for help in obtaining a 'commission by purchase' for his great nephew, Thomas.[76]

Stephen Nicholson died on 23rd February 1858 at the grand old age of eighty.

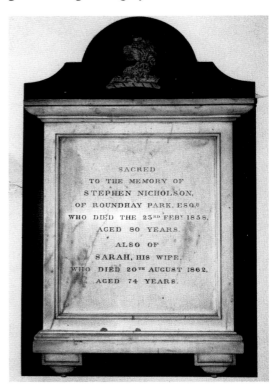

He was interred at the family vault of St. John's Church and an elaborate funeral monument was erected at the side of his step-brother's in the main body of the church.

He left everything 'to my dear wife in trust for my said nephew William Nicholson Nicholson', however, she was given five hundred pounds to distribute among his indoor and outdoor servants. His wife continued to live in the Mansion, her needs being tended to by a butler, footman, maid, cook and three house servants.[77] Gracious living indeed! Four years later she too was dead and William could, at long last, take charge of the estate.

A Family at War

William had much to be proud of, he had a wonderful family, a magnificent house, vast land holdings, a fortune in shares and as a Justice of the Peace was a respected and influential member of the community. Yet the seeds of the future family troubles were sown when his daughter, Emily, married William Armitage on 7 August 1860.[78] The Armitages of Farnley Hall were wealthy and respectable, though not quite of the same standing as Nicholsons. The courtship says a great deal about the social norms of the time. She recalled

We came from Manchester to Leeds in the train and stopped at Wortley station to have our tickets taken. There for the first time I saw my husband, he was reading a newspaper and waiting for a train to take him to Leeds.

Two days later when I got to Farnley I found that he was the one they called Mr Willie. I had been brought up in such simplicity that I felt rather shy of talking to the young Mr. Olivants and was not quite at my ease with him. As Mr Willie was old and with a bald head, I preferred being with him. We had such a happy fortnight.[79]

She visited Farnley several times and the couple became close, however, their parents failed to agree on how much money they would require to live on and so the matter was dropped. For five years they regularly met at social gatherings but were not allowed to speak to each other. This changed dramatically when Emily became godmother at a Harrogate christening. Her father said ' If you see Mr Willie you are quite at liberty to speak to him'.

This meeting led to her wedding. She leaves a delightful description of the event:

I was brought up to London for my trousseau and we went from one grand shop to another buying such a quantity of clothes. I had a very pretty white silk gown and a plain tulle veil with a wreath of orange-blossom round my head, and I had six bridesmaids.

The service was nicely performed; no hymns were sung in those days, so it was very quiet. There was another arch of roses near the church and the school children strewed my path with flowers. The bridegroom looked very ill.

The wedding breakfast was very grand, a special cook had been three days preparing it, and every dish had a little white flag on it. After this meal I very soon went to get dressed to go on my journey. I had a drab dress on, and a white shawl, and a blue bonnet trimmed with sky blue ribbon. I daresay it would look very old-fashioned now, but it looked very pretty then. We went to Chester that evening, and the next day to the Menai Straits.[80]

William Armitage became more than just a son in law, he became a confidante and trusted friend of William Nicholson Nicholson, to the extent that he was made one of his executors.

William Nicholson Nicholson was a decent man who tried to treat his children fairly. He appointed his wife, his friend William Fison, his cousin John Whitaker and son-in-law William Armitage executors of his will. This was a long and complex fourteen page document in which he clearly outlined his wishes. He died on the 19th September 1868 aged sixty four.

His funeral was an elaborate affair and he too was placed in the family vault at St. John's. A funeral monument was erected in the church to match those of his two uncles.

SACRED
TO THE MEMORY OF
WILLIAM NICHOLSON NICHOLSON,
OF ROUNDHAY PARK, ESQUIRE,
WHO DIED SEPTEMBER 19TH 1868,
AGED 64 YEARS.

ALSO OF
MARTHA, HIS WIFE,
WHO DIED AUGUST 26TH 1871,
AGED 61 YEARS.

His will was proved in London two months later. Martha was to receive £4000 for her immediate use. His farm bailiff, butler, housekeeper and head gardener were each given nineteen guineas and his coachman, George Smith, was to receive the sum of thirty pounds. Other indoor and outdoor servants received sums varying from five to ten pounds. This part was carried out with ease; however, unlike his uncles, William had numerous offspring, all of whom wished for a share of their father's wealth. The complex nature of his financial affairs, ranging from property to stocks and shares, meant that the sensible way forward was to sell everything and then divide the money between Martha, his children and a myriad of grandchildren.

His will states ' I give and bequeath all my manor or lordship of Roundhay, my Mansion House in Roundhay Park and all those freehold estates situate in Roundhay, Shadwell, Barwick-in-Elmet, Thorner, Whitkirk and Leeds and any real estate of whatever nature or kind to the executors and [they] shall

absolutely dispose of all the aforesaid real estate *when and so soon as it shall seem practicable so to do.'*[81] It was this final phrase that allowed certain of the executors to embark on what must be regarded as fraudulent activity. John Whitaker decided not to get embroiled in the family dispute and withdrew as an executor, leaving Martha isolated and vulnerable.

She argued that William Armitage, William Fison, her son, Walter Nicholson and son-in-law, Andrew Lawrence Busk, were deliberately delaying the sale of her husband's assets, while at the same time benefiting from the rents and profits. She inferred that they failed to keep accounts and regularly divided the spoils between them, thereby depriving the rest of the family of their inheritance. Despite Martha's protestations the four refused to organise the sale of assets and so, on 30th July 1869, ten months after her husband's death, she instructed Messrs Ewans and Foster of 2, Gray's Inn Square, London, to issue suit in the Court of Chancery.[82] The atmosphere can only be imagined. For her to take proceedings against her son, two sons in law and a family friend must have been both hurtful and embarrassing. Nevertheless, the Court found in her favour, allowing the affairs of William's estate to be administered by independent agents and accountants.

Hepper and Sons were immediately instructed to arrange the sale of the property. Jonathan Eddison, Land Agent and Surveyor, measured each room of the Mansion and prepared the necessary descriptions, while J. F. Masser and Son, Lithographers of Boar Lane, provided the illustrations.[83] Every villa, farm, field, barn and outbuilding were methodically listed in preparation for one of the most impressive sale catalogues ever produced in Leeds. This was to be a spectacular sale, one which would sever the Nicholson links with Roundhay forever.

The 1871 Sale Particulars extol the virtues of the district, describing it as *'the most charming suburb of Leeds, presenting a magnificent landscape unsullied by the smoke of the town, broken by hill and dale, adorned by rich Plantations and fine Parks, and studded with Gentlemen's Seats and Homesteads, which, meeting the eye at every turn, afford an amount of enjoyment seldom associated with so close a proximity to Leeds'.*[84] Yet who had enough money to purchase such a property? Hepper intimated that it might be of interest *'not only to gentlemen seeking residences but also to capitalists who may be desirous of profiting by its development'.*[85] One man had a radically different view.

The Mayor of Leeds, John Barran, believed that Roundhay would make an ideal park for the town, declaring:

'Here we have an estate which would make an ideal playground for the people of this town. Future generations will remember us with gratitude as they stroll along the pleasant walks and enjoy the ease and shade of the trees.' [86]

He lived at Chapel Allerton Hall, the former Nicholson property pictured below, miles away from the proposed park - a point not lost on the 'aristocracy of Roundhay', which comprised a number of wealthy merchants, manufacturers and professionals, including James Kitson, Francis Lupton, Henry Hudson, William Coopers Jagger, George Buckton, Henry Marshall Sykes and Henry Andrews.[87] The scheme enraged all of them. They totally abhorred the idea of hordes of working class people passing their gates and peering over their walls on the way to the park. This powerful group of men speedily organised themselves into an opposition group and fought hard - all the way to Parliament! But events were moving quickly, for the sale was to take place in October.

Barran faced other difficulties. Roundhay was a 'handsome rural village' over three miles to the north of the town. It lay outside the bounds of Leeds and current legislation limited the council to expending a mere £50,000 on a single item. It would require a special act of Parliament to permit its acquisition. There was no time to obtain one. Yet Barran persisted, and with the help of colleagues on the council, decided to purchase the land on behalf of the people of Leeds and obtain permission later. This was a risky strategy. However, civic pride may well have influenced Barran's decision.

John Barran

The previous year Bradford Corporation had obtained Lister Park. Leeds had Woodhouse Moor which the local paper derided as 'a standing disgrace, being little better than a foul quagmire, decorated by all the diseased cattle in the town.' [88] Surely Leeds could do better than this?

On 4th October 1871 John Barran made his way to Great Northern Station Hotel to bid for Lot 19 'consisting of a Noble Mansion, Carriage House, Stables, Entrance Lodges, Cottages, Homestead, Parks, Pleasure Grounds, Plantation and extensive Ornamental Waters' and adjoining Lot 20. [89] Barran had even re-mortgaged his home in order to raise enough money to bid! It was well known that a Manchester building speculator was very interested in the estate and so the atmosphere in the room was particularly tense. The bidding was swift and he eventually obtained both lots for £139,000.

Barran and his associates now owned the land. They immediately offered Lots 19 and 20 to the Town Council at cost, plus interest. The council accepted, providing that the necessary act could be obtained. The Roundhay élite now had the opportunity to scupper Barran's plans and they began a campaign of vociferous opposition to the Leeds Improvement Bill. This was viewed as a clear fight between the citizens of Leeds and the landowners of Roundhay.

A Park for Nothing

John Barran had been actively involved in the Boar Lane Improvement Scheme of 1868, which successfully widened the road from a mere twenty one feet to sixty six, and produced the impressive street with which we are familiar today. [90] The old properties were obtained using compulsory purchase orders, the buildings were speedily demolished, the road widened and then the building plots abutting the new road were auctioned off. The money obtained from the sale of these plots paid for the road widening scheme and so the people of Leeds benefited from a much improved road network at no cost.

Barran intended to apply a similar system at Roundhay. The idea was simple: 150 acres was to be retained as a public park, the farmland was to be let, while the remainder was to be sold for building land on which to erect high class villas. The money from the sale of the surplus land would pay for the public space and the people of Leeds gain a park for nothing! Barran envisaged the magnates of Leeds competing eagerly for sites.

James Kitson, the famous locomotive engineer, (pictured opposite), bitterly opposed such a plan. Six years earlier he had purchased Roundhay Lodge from the Nicholsons.

After demolishing the old mansion he had spent a fortune building a fashionable villa with extensive landscaped grounds and superb views across the town. He could not stomach the idea of his work people being allowed access to his perimeter fence. He spoke for many when he deplored the loss of seclusion and privacy and argued that Roundhay was far too distant from the homes of the operative classes. Kitson also feared that the opening of the park would lead to 'unseemly behaviour', while increased traffic would put a strain on local roads which the council had no duty to maintain. [91] The 'Roundhay aristocracy' also argued that the authority had no right to enter into such a large building speculation, and presented a petition to Parliament against the purchase.

An amusing poster (opposite) lampooning the Roundhay landowners was pasted throughout the streets of the town. It suggested that Victoria Square, the area in front of the Town Hall, was being cleared for the guillotine:

It was difficult for the council to communicate the beauties of the park to people so far distant in London. Eventually they commissioned Atkinson Grimshaw, the now famous local artist, to produce three paintings to provide the parliamentary commissioners with some idea of the park's appearance. Surprisingly night scenes were painted, however, Grimshaw excelled himself and this group of paintings proved to be among his finest. [93]

In 1865 James Kitson commissioned local architects John Dobson and Charles Chorley to design and build Elmet(e) Hall.

Popular support was mustered and huge rallies were held in the Coloured Cloth Hall Yard. People marched through the streets waving banners and singing popular songs accompanied by local bands.

Over 50,000 walked to the park on Whit Monday with twice that number making the long journey the following day. At 3 o'clock on 8th June 1872 the band of the 4th West Yorkshire led the 'Great People's Demonstration' through the streets, showing that the ratepayers of Leeds were definitely behind the scheme. The press reported this outpouring of public support in great detail.[94] The event was timed to perfection. It coincided with the difficult moment when the Leeds Improvement Bill reached the Select Committee. If passed, it would allow the council power to spend £150,000 on a recreation ground outside the bounds of the borough.

> CITIZENS,
>
> The COMMONS OF LEEDS, assembled in their Town Hall, DECIDE TO BUY ROUNDHAY PARK.
>
> The COMMONS OF ENGLAND, assembled in their House ENDORSE THIS DECISION.
>
> The ARISTOCRATS OF LEEDS petition against this Purchase.
>
> The ARISTOCRATS OF ENGLAND entertain this Petition.
>
> WHICH IS TO WIN THE DAY?
>
> A SCORE of Private Gentlemen in Leeds, and 300 Private Gentlemen in the Hereditary Chamber?
> or,
> a town with a QUARTER OF A MILLION INHABITANTS, and the Elected Representatives of a nation of 30 MILLIONS! [92]

Barran need not have worried. By the time the Bill came before the Select Committee, it was clear that the 'Roundhay Aristocracy' had lost. Mr. Denison Q.C., the council's barrister, quickly summarised the arguments for the purchase and emphasised that this was a unique opportunity for the 260,000 citizens of Leeds. He stressed that these people should have the right to enjoy the benefits of such a park, miles away from the smoke ladened skies of the town. He added:

Populations of this kind (should) have some place where fresh air could be obtained, where the people could see green trees and green fields, and if they could enjoy a sight of water so much the better ...because in Leeds trees absolutely refuse to grow. They had their pores choked with smoke from morning to night that they could not breathe; and while there was doubtless a certain amount of inconvenience in having a park at this distance, he ought to tell the committee that near Leeds there was no other place which could be made into a park. The River Aire ran through the town, and on the west the manufactories accompanied the river. He could remember great alterations in the aspect of the district, and in order to give the idea of the effect of smoke from the factories he might observe that in the surrounding countryside even the sheep were black.

(To which a noble lord added ... and some blue!)

The sheep might be divided into those two classes - black and blue - for young lambs were not allowed to be white for a few days. Of course as these manufactories extended up the river it became more and more impossible to provide anything like a park in that direction. East of Leeds the country soon ran into a coal field, and was flat country as well. To the south of Leeds the country was of much the same character. There remained therefore, only the north of Leeds, and practically only this part, because other land on the more immediate north was occupied by residences in such a way as to render it extremely unlikely that it would come onto the market.[95]

Such eloquent words helped win the day and the opposition could do little but acknowledge defeat. The Leeds Improvement Act received Royal Assent and Roundhay Park instantly became one of the largest municipal parks in the country - infinitely better than Bradford's!

This wonderful view of Waterloo Lake and the Lower Waterfall in 1872 shows that the park quickly became a place of resort for the well dressed middle classes.

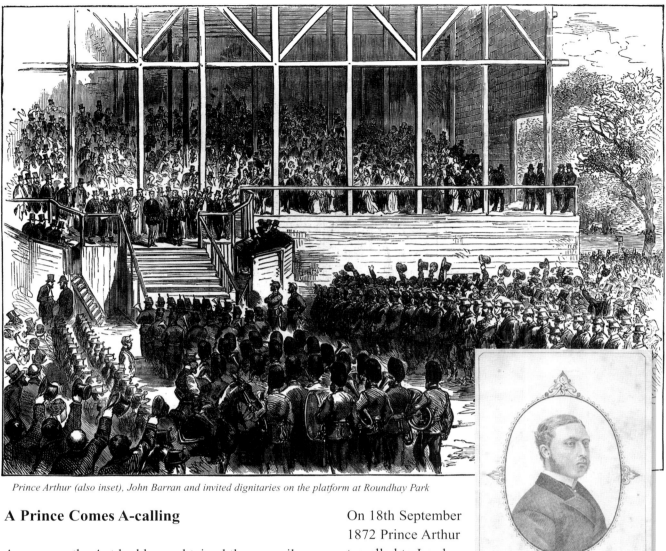

Prince Arthur (also inset), John Barran and invited dignitaries on the platform at Roundhay Park

A Prince Comes A-calling

As soon as the Act had been obtained the council arranged for the purchase of the property and began to make arrangements for the formal opening of the park. Prince Arthur, Queen Victoria's third son, agreed to perform the task. John Barran, Mayor of the town, was placed in charge of the arrangements with a budget of one thousand pounds.[96] This proved woefully inadequate and he was forced to ask for a further thousand. At this point a member of the opposition suggested that it would be cheaper if Barran opened it himself, adding that it was his park anyway! Throughout the bitter campaign opponents had accused Barran of buying the park in order to become 'Sir John', after all, when Queen Victoria came to open the Town Hall in 1858, a highlight of that visit had been the bestowing of a knighthood on the Mayor, Peter Fairbairn![97] If this had been one of Barran's motives he was to be bitterly disappointed.

On 18th September 1872 Prince Arthur travelled to Leeds and stayed at Harewood House. The following day the Prince's party made a triumphant entrance into the town and arrived at the Town Hall for eleven thirty, where he was greeted by the Mayor. After a short reception in the Town Hall the Prince, escorted by the Yorkshire Hussars, and followed by a long train of civic dignitaries, made his way to the park.

He was shown the Mansion and then taken on a short walk to view the Upper Lake, before following the path down to the Old Castle. The party then returned and took their places on the specially erected platform. After a short speech Barran invited the Prince to declare the park officially open, after which the party retired to the marquee to enjoy a special luncheon, served with 'great elegance' by Mr Powolny of Commercial Street, Leeds.[98]

There were great celebrations in the town and cheap mementoes of the event were either given away or sold by shopkeepers and street venders.

However, it was John Middlebrook, in the Bramley Almanac, who accurately foretold the future:

Hurrah for Barran! what d'ye think abaght wer Mayor nah?
Three cheers for Barran! upwi t'cap an shaat ageaan hurrah
He's gam is t'lad! Come what's to think be what he's dun t'day
Wah, it dussant matter much to me bud - somb'dy'll hev to pay!

It's t'grandest place - thah never saw, owd lad, a place so nice!
Thah shak's thi head it's true, I knaw, its a longish price;
But then it's nowt for Leeds - they can rise it onny day
Can they? Well its reight to me, bud - sumb'dy'll hev to pay!

Hey up for Leeds! I dunnot care hah big is t'debt at's on!
We've gotton a rattlin paairk at last, - all thanks to thee, Sir John
It can't be bet all England throo - at least so judges say
An it isn't all that can't be bet! - there's a rattlin debt to pay! -

They were prophetic words! [99]

C. Goodall.   THE GLEN, ROUNDHAY PARK.   Leeds.

An artist's impression of 1876 showing how the villa sites at Roundhay could be developed, based on a view of the area drawn from the top of The Mansion.

W. MABERLY DEL.

How to Develop the Park?

Now the park was officially open the Council had a duty to ratepayers to speedily sell off the surplus land. They urgently needed a master plan that identified the areas for villa development but ensured that these did not impinge on the beauties of the park. Moreover, the grounds themselves needed attention. More roads, footpaths and rustic bridges, besides new features like bandstands, croquet lawns and summerhouses were required to create a modern Victorian park.[100] What to do with the Mansion itself? Some suggested it should be a museum, others an official residence for the mayor; the legal establishment favoured its use for Her Majesty's Judges of Assize, while the Temperance Party insisted that if it became a hotel, alcohol should not be served. Professional advice had to be obtained. As so often happened in such circumstances the Council decided to hold a competition with a first prize of £500.[101] George Corson's plan was deemed to be the most imaginative. His ambitious plans, dated 1873, included boathouses, refreshment rooms, lodges, a swimming bath and cricket ground.

This he felt could be achieved for around £36,000. However, the park had already cost a fortune and none of this work could be undertaken without the sale of the surplus land.

Illustration 19 from George Corson's winning design entry of 1873.

Corson's plan identified two large areas for development. The first centred on Spring Wood to the south east, the other along the western boundary, beyond Old Park Road.

Illustration 17 from George Corson's winning design entry of 1873.

More controversial was the laying out of Park Avenue, leading from Oakwood towards Waterloo Lake, and West Avenue along the hill. Land sales were held at intervals but building restrictions, including the use of stone and the prohibition of any noisy or offensive trade, were scrupulously enforced. This ensured that it would be an area of quality housing,

The land sales were crucial to the success of the Council's strategy and they went to extraordinary lengths to interest potential buyers in the auction sales. They even hired an artist to sit on the roof of the Mansion and create an artist's impression (Page 33) of what the area would look like if the villa development went ahead as envisaged.[102]

Unfortunately, the long distance from town and the complete lack of reliable public transport meant that the Council had few takers. Auction sales in 1876 and 1877 disposed of about sixty acres, but many lots were withdrawn. No sales at all were made in 1879 and, much to their embarrassment, large swathes of land were to remain unsold for years.[103]

Yet again the Barran family acted as a shining example to other members of the middle class élite and in 1883 a large house called Parcmont (below) was constructed near the lake for John Barran II. Though other substantial houses were built, the overall strategy proved to be a disaster.[104]

The park had cost the ratepayers of Leeds a fortune.

Parcmont by the noted architect Thomas Ambler.

An aerial view of 1929 showing how the area abutting Park Avenue actually developed.

The White Elephant

It was now that the real drawback to its acquisition became plain and that was its distance from the centre and the people who owned it. Roundhay was remote in 1872, reached only by the old turnpike road completed in 1810. Its distance from Leeds discouraged many from making the journey on foot, while cabs and 'buses were prohibitively expensive for 'ordinary folk'. Poor transport links combined with a six day working week, meant that it was impossible for most working class people to visit the park. It became an exclusive haven for the middle class.

Low attendance figures and disappointing land sales supported the view held all along by Barran's opponents, that the park was too far from Leeds and that the Council should not have concerned itself with speculative building projects. The proposed railway scheme foundered and there was a complete failure to provide adequate means of public transport.

Barran faced increasing criticism and nick-names for the park such as 'Barran's Folly' and 'The White Elephant' reflected the change in the public's perception of him. This process was hastened by the publication of humorous pamphlets, one of the most effective being 'The Big White Elephant' published in 1879. It accurately reflected the ratepayers frustrations:

*The White Elephant is published with the desire to calling the ratepayers attention to the reckless waste of their money, which in spite of hard times is wrung from them by paying interest on 500 acres of surplus land not required for the park. The whole estate is grossly mismanaged. The bait was magnificent. The Park was bought - A prince sent like a flash of lightning to open it ...we went half wild with delight - 'A Prince and a Park for nothing! Gorgeous illusion! Splendid dream! But the awakening after seven years' sleep, dead loss of sixty thousand pounds, and an annual loss of four thousand pounds which was to have paid for the park - a **barren** result indeed.*[105]

In 1882 another scurrilous publication 'Leeds Made Uglier' by Eli Pitchin appeared, complete with cartoons and a damning text. It highlighted other aspects of the Council's mismanagement:

There was no water, very few seats, no sheltering places, no sanitary accommodation for ladies - nothing but a few stinking wood sheds swarming with insect life, where the most disgusting practices were in vogue, until at length the Local Government Board instituted an inquiry, and are now compelling the Corporation to erect decent retiring places for ladies.[106]

The humorous advertisements lampooned the Council for its failure to solve the key problems.

LOST EIGHTY THOUSAND POUNDS and upwards, at Roundhay Park by the Ratepayers of Leeds. Anyone finding the same please restore it to the Corporate Property Committee.

WANTED TO KNOW why the two and a quarter million square yards of Surplus Land, north of the Park, are not offered for sale. Any person having land, horticultural or otherwise, to dispose of , please offer direct to the White Elephant Committee, Town Hall, Leeds.

Wanted a number of persons to join in getting up a BALLOON ROUTE to Roundhay Park, as by no other method can the public be so well accommodated. Sure to pay.

Special criticism continued to be aimed at John Barran himself, with Eli claiming 'It was a gem of a Park when purchased by Mr. Barran ten years ago; but since then the 'concentrated intelligence' has been improving it uglier day by day'.[107] Such comments were extremely hurtful. Barran tried to fend off further criticism by addressing one of the public's many complaints - the lack of drinking water.

He commissioned the architect Thomas Ambler to design an elegant drinking fountain for the park. Ambler excelled himself and produced a fine rotunda with eight classical columns. Inside the dome was the inscription 'Presented to Leeds Corporation by John Barran, M.P. 3rd April 1882'.[108] Twenty taps connected directly to the town's water supply from Eccup, provided continuous free refreshment for the thirsty visitor, while the waste was caught beneath in expensive red granite basins. Today it remains one of the most beautiful features of the park, a lasting memorial to a 'man of vision'.

The Super Tram

In 1871 Roundhay still had only 583 inhabitants. Many of the wealthy residents owned carriages, so demand for public transport was limited. For over twenty years John Machan had run a regular bus to Leeds and Scarcroft, which more than satisfied demand, but the opening of the park to the public radically changed the situation. Machan supplemented his meagre service at weekends with innumerable wagonettes and cabs, but this was grossly inadequate.[109]

John Barran was in favour of constructing a railway to Roundhay and in 1874 helped to found the 'Leeds, Roundhay and Osmondthorpe Railway Company'. Unfortunately the scheme failed to gain public support and on 6th February 1877, Barran finally acknowledged defeat, noting that many had held back because of the seasonal nature of demand and the feeling that the railway should have connected Moortown and Headingley.[110]

In the meantime wagonettes, omnibuses and a myriad of other vehicles provided a chaotic service to Roundhay. Many were unsafe. On 10th August 1875 one lucky survivor of a wagonette crash wrote to the Yorkshire Post warning fellow readers of the hidden hazards of travelling to and from the park on such vehicles. He related in lurid detail the series of events that led to the accident but concluded that it was the condition of one of the brakes that was to blame, for it *'seemed almost worn through, while an old slipper or shoe tied with a piece of string was used as a substitute'.*[111]

Road improvements were made. In 1878 unemployed men were put to work on constructing a new section of road from Oakwood to the Canal Gardens. This became known as Prince's Avenue, named after Prince Arthur who had opened the park six years earlier. It allowed visitors far easier access to the Mansion and the western end of the park. Park Avenue was constructed around the same time.[112]

At holiday periods almost all buses in Leeds were withdrawn from their regular routes to cope with the demand. Street arabs and urchins lined the route, badgering passengers for a penny in return for performing somersaults and other tricks. The situation was farcical. Even more irritating for many working class people of the town was the fact that middle class families from outside the borough regularly visited the park. The fares still made it prohibitively expensive for 'ordinary folk' even to get to the park they owned. Something radical had to be done.

Arguably the most ambitious scheme was submitted to the Council in 1887. This was an elevated railway, a system recently patented by two Leeds engineers, J. Clark Jefferson and J.T. Pullon. This monorail was very similar to the one in Chicago and was nick-named 'The Tight Rope Railway'. The line was to consist of a single rail on lattice girder. The nine ton engine would draw eight to ten carriages at a top speed of 25 miles per hour. Each carriage would be capable of holding up to thirty two people.[113] Supporters argued that it would be safer, quicker and have cheaper operating costs than other proposed solutions.

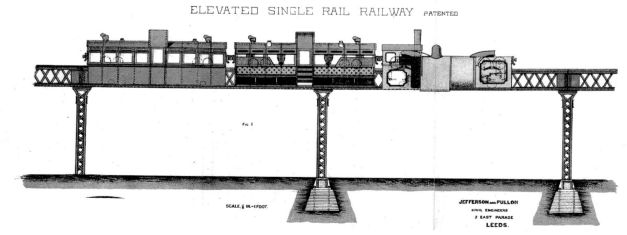

ELEVATED SINGLE RAIL RAILWAY PATENTED

Unfortunately this visionary scheme received little support from Council members, who were concerned about high initial costs, the unsightly nature of the girders and the potential noise problems. Despite the offer to build banks and plant tall trees the scheme was rejected.

Eventually, on 29th September 1887, after much heated discussion, the Council voted for a provisional order to construct a tramway. Since 1871 The Tramways Company had had a monopoly to run such services in Leeds, yet the Highways Committee foolishly failed to reach agreement with them before embarking on the necessary road widening, which took place between December 1888 and February 1889. The first tram ran successfully from Sheepscar to Roundhay Park on 3rd August 1889 but the shortcomings of the new system were quickly highlighted two days later, when the rain hardly stopped and the trams failed to grip on the slippery rails. At each rise in the ground the conductor had to throw sand in front of the steam tram in order to make the wheels bite![114]

Further complications arose when the Council, who owned the line failed to reach an agreement with The Tramway Company and, as a result of the stalemate, no trams ran for nearly two years. Salvation came on 10th September 1890 when the Highways Committee received a letter from C.H. Wilkinson of the Thomson-Houston International Company expressing interest in running an electric tramcar route to Roundhay Park.[115]

A Thomson-Houston car at Roundhay terminus c. 1892.

Negotiations went well and on 13th May 1891 an agreement was signed between the two parties and The Tramway Company agreed to run a temporary service. Once again civic pride rose to the fore when it was pointed out that this would be the first electric tramway operating on the overhead wire system in Europe. So, at one o'clock on 29th October 1891, senior members of Leeds Council, along with dignitaries from all the nearby towns, gathered at the Sheepscar terminus to witness the formal opening of the line. Local journalists, who had for years reported on the constant wrangling over the Roundhay line, were there to pass judgment. Nearly an hour and a half passed before the tramcars appeared, by which time several councillors and other 'worthy' visitors had left in disgust. There had been a problem raising enough power. The invited guests embarked on the six tramcars and at long last the mayor, Alf Cooke, released the lever of the first vehicle. The procession finally began to move towards the park. Unfortunately, just before the Harehills junction, the power failed and the trams stopped. Councillor Atha remarked that nothing would please him better than to have the 'buses come and pick them up to convey them back to town! Seventeen minutes later the cars moved again but after only a couple of hundred yards the vehicles ground to a halt once more. This time there was a half hour delay, by which time many irate guests had walked back to town. Eventually the trams reached the park entrance. The journey had taken one hour ten minutes! The special luncheon prepared for the guests had gone cold and the day ended with cutting remarks in the press.[116]

Despite these teething troubles the line proved immensely popular with the general public and in the next five years over four million passengers travelled by electric tram to Roundhay. On 31st July 1896 the Council took over the line directly and work began on the extension of the line to the Canal Gardens. Thomson-Houston withdrew their electric cars and the Council introduced steam cars as a temporary measure.

The official opening of the Kirkstall and Roundhay tramway, 29 July 1897.

On 29th July 1897 Sir James Kitson, Lord Mayor of Leeds officially opened the new Kirkstall - Roundhay Electric Tramway.[117] The problem of getting the people of Leeds to Roundhay Park had been solved.

The People's Park

At long last the masses could reach the park and its increasing popularity encouraged the Council to invest in a range of new amenities. In 1894 a vast sports arena was constructed, providing work for a large number of unemployed. Cycle racing was at its zenith and a grass cycling track was built around the periphery providing modern facilities for enthusiasts.[118] The arena was regularly used to host charity cricket matches and nearly twenty years later it was even offered as a venue for the F.A.Cup Final!

Magnificent entrance gates, pathways and formal flower beds were constructed in the area between the Mansion and the Canal Gardens. These wonderful gardens became a source of civic pride, a place of resort for thousands who lived in the smoke-filled streets of back-to-back houses in the city and who flocked there in their thousands every Saturday afternoon and Sunday.

In January 1904, a reporter from *The Gardeners' Chronicle* wrote ecstatically about the floral displays at Roundhay, praising the originality and ability of the superintendent:

The old formal stereotyped methods of flower bedding have been entirely superseded by a more artistic and natural one of massing together suitable flowering plants, but interspersing them with some well-known plants of the sub - tropical kind.[119]

The new boathouse after its completion in June 1902.

The lake was another draw. Leeds and District Anglers leased the rights from the Council and many tried their skill at fishing for pike, perch and roach. Others preferred the more sedate pleasure of 'a trip around the lake'.

In 1907 the unemployed were once again busy, this time constructing a bathing pool just below the main dam of Waterloo Lake.[122] This proved to be another popular attraction.

A steam boat called 'The Maid of Athens' sailed the waters of the lake for many years before a brand new steamer, 'The Mary Gordon' was launched in 1899, named after the Lady Mayoress of the time. In 1902 Council workers completed a new boathouse on the western edge of Waterloo Lake, with storage for one hundred and fifty boats. To the eastern side was a dry dock for 'The Mary Gordon'.[121]

In 1911 the Council demolished the old conservatory in the former Kitchen Garden and constructed the Coronation House as an elegant display conservatory. The following year Roundhay became the venue for the Leeds Horticultural Society's annual show. This quickly became a regular feature of the park's calendar of events and twenty years later crowds of over fifteen thousand people made their annual pilgrimage to view the contents of the elegant marquees upon Soldiers' Field.[120]

The Open Air Swimming Pool opening on 19 June 1907.

40

However, by 1932 it was in an appalling state and one person felt compelled to berate the Council for the state of the facilities:

The water is never clean, and it is impossible to see the rough bottom of the bath. Dead flies float about at the shallow end of the pool. The surrounding path is covered with sand - bathers carry it into the pool with them. As there is no footpath it is easy to see why the water becomes so dirty. It is an eyesore and a disgrace.[123]

It was virtually rebuilt in 1937 and between 80,000 to 120,000 people used the baths each year throughout the late Fifties and early Sixties.

The park was a resounding success and became the main outdoor venue for a wide range of spectacular extravaganzas. These were often organised to raise money for worthy causes like hospitals or children's charities. The Military Tattoo became a regular attraction. In 1906 some six hundred soldiers of the Leeds Rifles took part. The regiment was divided into four squads who waited at different locations around the park for the proceedings to begin. At nine o'clock hundreds of coloured rockets were launched into the night sky as a signal for the troops to make their way to the arena, accompanied by military bands playing stirring music. After the drills came a military tournament by the Yorkshire Hussars.[124] Unfortunately on 25th June 1910 the Leeds Lifeboat Gala was marred when, in the opening movements of the Military Tattoo, a bombshell, intended to signal the arrival of the troops, prematurely exploded in the mortar, killing two and seriously injuring a further six people. The military regularly used the park and from the end of the nineteenth century troops marched from Chapeltown Barracks to train in the area now known as Soldiers' Field.[125]

The spoils of war were even displayed in marquees at a special Aircraft Exhibition staged on the 18th and 19th June 1919.[126] These specially staged displays had people flocking to the park and the Military Tattoo of 10th July 1926 drew a crowd of over 130,000 people! [127]

A close competitor for visitor numbers was Children's Day which, throughout the Thirties and Forties, regularly attracted over 100,000 people to watch what today might seem a rather tame programme of events. Children's Day started back in 1920 as a modest outing for school children and grew to become one of the most influential social events of its time.

Children's Day, Saturday 26 June 1939 where 2,000 school boys formed 'a wonderful display of exercises'.

Three teachers, Vernon Harrison, Archie Gordon and Arthur Thornton were concerned that many pupils never left the confines of their immediate surroundings. They came up with the idea of an annual outing to Roundhay Park, with organised games, fancy dress competition and picnic.

The Yorkshire Evening Post helped to publicise the event and organise 'The Bonnie Baby Competition'. Judges were astonished at the thousands of entries they received - the finalists being transported to Roundhay Park in an expensive limousine as part of the Children's Day procession.[128]

In 1923 artists from The Empire, Hippodrome and City Varieties gave open-air performances to the delighted crowds. Swimming and water games were held on Waterloo Lake and well known sports personalities made guest appearances. Children's Day quickly established itself as an annual event. A highlight of the day was the crowning of the 'Queen of the May', who arrived in the arena by car, accompanied by her attendants. Schools began to do more, preparing mass physical education and dancing displays. At a time of austerity this simple but effective form of entertainment brought pleasure to thousands. In 1949 the event was held twice, a 'special edition' being staged for Princess Elizabeth and Prince Philip. By the early Sixties many felt the event appeared dated and the dreadful weather of 1963 hastened its demise.[129] Shortly afterwards bad weather was again blamed for the end of the wonderful Bank Holiday Galas which the Council had been running since 1947.[130] Nevertheless, staff continued to think of new and exciting ways of using the park.

Ice skaters on the Upper Lake during the winter of 1958.

In 1977 the first free municipal bonfire proved to be a success attracting vast numbers to view the magnificent firework displays in complete safety.[131]

Perhaps the most controversial use of Roundhay Park was for pop concerts. These centred on the sports arena but huge areas had to be fenced off to keep out those without tickets. Despite understandable opposition from local residents the Council allowed several concerts to take place, arguing that the income could then be spent on improving facilities at Roundhay. In 1982 a crowd of over 80,000 people watched The Rolling Stones and helped raise over £63,000 for the city. Bruce Springsteen (1985), Genesis (1987 & 92), Madonna (1987), Michael Jackson (1988 & 92), Simple Minds (1989) and U2 (1997) are just some of the world class performers who have appeared at Roundhay.[132]

In 1983 one of the most spectacular additions was made to the attractions at Roundhay. The popular Coronation House had already been rebuilt once, in 1939, but by the late Seventies it was in a poor condition. Imaginative plans were formulated to expand and modernise the structure This became known as 'Tropical World' and contained a wide variety of rare and unusual plants, with the pools forming a sanctuary for some endangered species of fish. Butterflies, insects, birds and small mammals became another exciting feature of this area. By 1990 it was number seven in the list of British wildlife attractions and three years later was once again extended due to the generosity of a local benefactor. In 1998 it was voted 'Top Garden Venue of the Year' and had become the nation's second biggest tourist attraction, a testimony to the skill and devotion of the dedicated staff who labour hard to make it such a beautiful place to visit.[133]

The new Millennium began with a generous grant of over six million pounds from the Heritage Lottery Fund to help restore and conserve the park.

The Coronation House and Tropical World. The original Coronation House was constructed in 1911 on the site of an earlier conservatory. Named to commemorate the coronation of George V, it was rebuilt in 1939 and modernised again in 1984. Tropical World opened on 7th May 1988 and was further extended in 1993.

Roundhay Park is constantly changing, yet the grounds of this former deer enclosure, so cleverly transformed by Thomas Nicholson, continue to give pleasure to millions of people who visit each year.

When John Barran was fighting to obtain the park he argued

'Future generations will remember us with gratitude as they stroll along the pleasant walks and enjoy the ease and shade of the trees.' [134]

How true that statement has proved to be.

References

1. Steven Burt and Kevin Grady, *An Illustrated History of Leeds* (Derby, 1994) pp. 10-29.
2. Susan Neave, *Medieval Parks of East Yorkshire* (Beverley, 1991) pp.5-10.
3. W.T.Lancaster and W.P.Baildon, ed., *Coucher Book of Kirkstall Abbey*, Thoresby Soc., Vlll (Leeds, 1904) pp.50-51.
4. This section of exposed ditch is just west of Roundhay Grange Farm but is on private land.
5. John W. Morkill, *The Manor and Park of Roundhay*, Thoresby Soc. (Leeds, 1893) (hereafter, Morkill) p.20. Note that this was a reprint of the same article which originally appeared in Thoresby Soc ll, Miscellany l (Leeds, 1891) and the page numbers in brackets refer to the original volume.
6. West Yorkshire Metropolitan County Council, *West Yorkshire: An Archaeological Survey to A.D.1500* (Wakefield, 1981) p.646.
7. John Cummins, *The Hound and The Hawk - The Art of Medieval Hunting* (1988).
8. Morkill p.20. (p.230)
9. W(est) Y(orkshire) A(rchive) S(ervice) DB/M242.
10. K. Harrison, trans., *Sir Gawain and the Green Knight* (1983) pp.57-67.
11. William Wheater, *Old Yorkshire*, 2nd Series (Leeds, 1885) p.187.
12. Morkill p.20. (p.230) *He mistakenly transcribed thackstone as chakstone (? chalkstone).
13. Ibid p.22. (p.232)
14. Ibid p.23.(p.233)
15. John Le Patourel, ed., *The Manor and Borough of Leeds, 1066-1400*, Thoresby Soc., XLV (Leeds, 1957) p.76.
16. Morkill pp.21-24. (pp.231-234)
17. Joan W. Kirby, ed., *The Manor and Borough of Leeds, 1425-1662*, Thoresby Soc., LVll (Leeds, 1983) p.30 and p.36.
18. G.D.Barnes, *Kirkstall Abbey, 1147-1539: An Historical Study*, Thoresby Soc., LVlll (Leeds, 1984) pp.6-16.
19. W.T.Lancaster and W.P.Baildon, ed., *Coucher Book of Kirkstall Abbey*, Thoresby Soc., Vlll (Leeds, 1904) pp.50-7.
20. Catherine Verna, *Les Mines et les forges des Cisterciens* (Paris,1995).
21. W.Dugdale, *Monasticon Anglicanum*, V (1846) pp.535-6.
22. R.A.Mott, *Kirkstall Forge and Monkish Iron-making*, Thoresby Soc., Vol. 53 (Leeds, 1972) p.157.
23. Stephen Moorhouse, *Medieval Iron Production* (Bolton Percy, 1980) and WYAS DB/M242.
24. E.K.Clark, ed., *The Foundation of Kirkstall Abbey*, Thoresby Soc. IV (Leeds, 1895) pp 204-205.
25. Barnes p.43-44.
26. Public Record Office - Ministers' Accounts for 1295-6 - Bundle 1, No.1.
27. F.S.Colman, *A History of the Parish of Barwick-in-Elmet*, Thoresby Soc., XVll (Leeds, 1908) p.263.
28. Morkill p.25. (p.235)
29. W.T.Lancaster, *Fifteenth Century Rentals of Barwick and Scholes*, Thoresby Soc., XXVlll (Leeds, 1928) pp.239-40.
30. Information supplied by Stephen Moorhouse.
31. Morkill pp.29-30. (pp.239-240)
32. WYAS Acc.1874: Copy of the 1628 Corporation of London Survey.
33. Kirby p.276.
34. Morkill pp.23-4. (pp.233-234)
35. Kirby p.278.
36. Ibid p.33-34.
37. Burt and Grady, p.34.
38. WYAS Acc. 1874 p.58.
39. Morkill p.33. (p.233)
40. Colman p.264.
41. Yorkshire Archaeological Society Archive MD279: Armitage Manuscripts
42. WYAS DB/M242.
43. Norma C. Neill, *The Elam Family: Quaker Merchants of England and America* (Doncaster, 1995) pp.75-7.
44. Ibid pp.96-7.
45. R.G.Wilson, *Gentlemen Merchants: The Merchant Community in Leeds 1700-1830* (Manchester, 1971) p. 205.
46. Joan Newiss, *The Mysteries of Roundhay Park*, Yorkshire Archaeological Society, Local History Study Section Bulletin No.39 (Leeds, 1998) pp.11-15.
47. Leeds Family & Local History Library ML1810.
48. Norma C. Neill, *The Elam Family: Quaker Merchants of England and America* (Doncaster, 1995) pp.97-98.
49. Joan Newiss, *Goodman House, Roundhay: A Detective Story*, Yorkshire Archaeological Society, Local History Study Section Bulletin No. 36 (Leeds, 1995) pp.25-29.
50. R.G.Wilson, *Gentlemen Merchants: The Merchant Community in Leeds 1700-1830* (Manchester, 1971) p. 205; Edward Baines, *History, Directory and Gazetteer of the County of York* (Leeds, 1822) p.584.
51. Neville Hurworth, *Thomas Nicholson of Roundhay Park*, unpublished article.
52. Doreen Newlyn, *This Goodly House - Its People and Its Times* (Leeds, 1998) pp. 98-99.
53. West Riding Register of Deeds GD 642.727.
54. *Kelly's Directory of Leeds and its Neighbourhood* (Leeds, 1899) p.25.
55. *Yorkshire Post*, 27 Feb. 1941.
56. Land Use Consultants, *Roundhay Park: A Landscape Restoration Management Plan* (Leeds, 1999) p.5.
57. WYAS DB/M523 Plan 1871.
58. *Leeds Intelligencer*, 23 and 30 Nov. 1812.
59. Frank Beckwith, *Thomas Taylor: Regency Architect, Leeds*, Thoresby Society Monograph 1. (Leeds, 1949) pp.30-1.
60. W.C.E. Hartley, *Banking in Yorkshire* (1975) and R.V. Taylor, *Biographia Leodiensis* (Leeds, 1865) p.461. Quaker reference, Neville Hurworth, *Thomas Nicholson of Roundhay Park*, unpublished article.
61. WYAS DB/M523 Plan 1871.
62. WYAS DB/39/18.
63. Beckwith p.65.
64. *Leeds Intelligencer*, 23 Sept.1824.
65. *Leeds Intelligencer*, 19 June 1826.
66. W.H.Scott, *St.John's Roundhay, Centenary 1826-1926* (Leeds, 1927); Jack Dickinson and Gilbert D.Webster, *A History of St. John's Church, Roundhay* (Leeds, 1967).
67. Public Record Office: Warrant Book HO 38/26.
68. James Rusby, Pedigrees and Arms of Leeds Families, Manuscript -Leeds Local and Family History Library.
69. *Yorkshire Evening Post*, 19 Sept.1972.
70. *Leeds Intelligencer*, 23 May 1840.
71. *Leeds Mercury*, 23 May 1840.
72. Ibid.
73. *Yorkshire Evening Post*, 19 Sept 1972.
74. Ibid.
75. *Yorkshire Evening Post*, 20 Sept. 1972.
76. Public Record Office: War Office 31/924 & 989
77. 1851 Census: Leeds Local and Family History Library Bundle No.2316 1st Reel Fol.147-163.

78. WYAS, Leeds, St.John's Parish Register: Marriages 1837-1902, p.93/2/2.

79. *Yorkshire Evening Post*, 20 Sept. 1972.

80. Ibid.

81. Will of William Nicholson Nicholson, Probate: PR 21 Nov. 1868.

82. Public Record Office: Chancery Proceedings - Pleadings 1861-75/ C16/591/N46 also C33/1157.

83. WYAS DB/M523 Plan 1871 and AM Sale Particulars (Series 1) 6624.

84. Hepper Plans 28 Sept.1870 at Leeds Local and Family History Library LF 333.333 H411.

85. Ibid.

86. *Yorkshire Evening Post Special Supplement*, 19 Sept.1972.

87. Janet Douglas, Chris Hammond and Ken Powell, *Leeds: Three Suburban Walks - No.6*, (Leeds, n.d.) p.27.

88. *Leeds Mercury*, 30 Sept. 1871.

89. *Leeds Intelligencer*, 5 Oct. 1871.

90. Brian Barber, *Municipal Government in Leeds*, 1835-1914, in Municipal Reform and the Industrial City ed., Derek Fraser (Leicester, 1982) pp.83-5.

91. Douglas, Hammond and Powell p.27.

92. Derek Linstrum, *West Yorkshire Architects and Architecture* (1978) p.121.

93. Alexander Robertson, *Atkinson Grimshaw* (Oxford, 1988) pp.34-38.

94. *Leeds Mercury Weekly Supplement*, 8 June 1872.

95. *Leeds Mercury Weekly Supplement*, 20 June 1872.

96. Charles Goodall, *Illustrated Royal Handbook* (Leeds, 1872) pp. 4-5.

97. Dorothy Payne, *The Queen's Visit to Leeds*, 1858 (Leeds, n.d.).

98. *Illustrated London News*, 28 Sept,1872 p.307.

99. John Middlebrook, *Bramley Almanac for 1872*

100. Douglas Taylor, *West Riding Amusement Parks and Gardens*, Yorkshire Archaeological Journal, Vol. 58 (Leeds, 1986) pp.179-184.

101. George Corson, Roundhay Park as proposed to be laid out and adapted - an illustrated plan, Leeds Local and Family History Library - QLR 76 (712).

102. WYAS, Leeds, AM Sale Particulars (Series 1) 665.

103. Barber pp.78-80.

104. Thoresby Society: Sale Particulars:1911 - Parcmont.

105. Charles Goodall, *The Big White Elephant* (Leeds, 1879).

106. Eli Pitchin, *Leeds Made Uglier* (Leeds, 1882).

107. Ibid p.22.

108. *Yorkshire Post*, 4 April 1882.

109. J.Soper, *Leeds Transport Vol.1. 1830 -1902* (Leeds, 1985) p.78.

110. *Yorkshire Post*, 10 Aug. 1875; Leeds Acts of Parliament Vol. 4. 8 June 1874;17 May 1877.

111. Soper p.80.

112. Derek Linstrum, *West Yorkshire Architects and Architecture* (1978) pp.121-3.

113. J. Clark Jefferson and J.T. Pullan, *A Description of the Proposed Elevated Single Rail Railway to Roundhay Park* (Leeds, 1887).

114. Soper pp.87-8.

115. Ibid p.90.

116. *Yorkshire Post*, 30 Oct. 1891.

117. Soper pp.127-8.

118. Arthur Elton, Leeds Cyclists and Cycle Makers, 1880-1901, Thoresby Soc. 2ND Series Vol. 5 (Leeds, 1995) pp.110-140.

119. The Gardeners Chronicle, Jan. 1904 pp.68-9.

120. W.S.Maney, Roundhay and Chapel Allerton Residential Handbooks (Leeds 1911-5).

121. *Yorkshire Evening Post*, 11 Nov.1972.

122. *Yorkshire Post*, 20 July 1907.

123. Quoted in *Yorkshire Evening Post Special Supplement*, 19 Sept. 1972.

124. *Yorkshire Evening News*, 6 July 1906.

125. *Yorkshire Post*, 26 June 1910.

126. *Yorkshire Post*, 11 July 1926.

127. *Yorkshire Post*, 18,19 and 20 July 1919.

128. Susan Green, *Leeds Children's Day* (Leeds, 1995).

129. *Roundhay Park Centenary 1872-1972: Souvenir Brochure* (Leeds, 1972) p.6.

130. Ibid pp.3-5.

131. *Yorkshire Evening Post*, 6 Nov. 1977.

132. For details regarding these concerts see Leeds Local and Family History Library Newspaper Cuttings Index.

133. *North Leeds Weekly Post*, 30 Oct.1998.

134. *Leeds Mercury*, 14 Oct. 1871.

Acknowledgements

I wish to thank Dr. Tony Moyes for his help with the medieval section and in particular for sharing over forty years of practical experience in methods of iron production, for translating the Latin documents in the Coucher Book of Kirkstall Abbey and for his companionship on our field-walking excursions. Special thanks go to Joan Newiss, who shared a wealth of information on Roundhay with me and who kindly commented on an early draft of the book. I am extremely grateful to June Underwood, who provided a range of original source material on the Nicholson family, Pauline Robson for work on their family tree and to Neville Hurworth, who gave me access to a copy of his unpublished article on 'Thomas Nicholson of Roundhay Park'.

I am particularly indebted to the Staff of Leeds Local and Family History Library, Leeds Museums and Galleries and West Yorkshire District Archive Service, Leeds. I also received most valuable assistance at other libraries and record offices including the Thoresby Society, the Leeds Library, the Yorkshire Archaeological Society, Leeds Civic Hall, the Royal Armouries, the West Yorkshire County Record Office and the West Yorkshire Archaeology Service, Wakefield.

The quality of this book was greatly enhanced by the superb photographic work of Dave Sheard and the imaginative graphic design by Phil Jewitt of the Graphics and Communications Group, Department of Planning and Environment, Leeds City Council.

Special thanks to Don Cole and Jean Mortimer for their positive comments and meticulous attention to detail. I greatly valued the constructive comments made by Kevin Grady, who actually took the final draft on holiday with him!

Dedicated to my wife, Lynda, whose love, patience and encouragement ensured that I actually finished this book.

Sources of Illustrations

Thanks are due to the following bodies, societies and individuals who have kindly granted permission to reproduce their material. Illustrations not listed below are in the author's collection.

Thoresby Society: Roundhay Grange, The Elevated Single Railway, Chapel Allerton Hall, The Glen and the exterior view of Elmete Hall.

West Yorkshire Archive Service: Leeds: Jonathan Taylor's Plan of 1803 - DB/M 242. Villa Sites: AM Sale Particulars (series 1) 665.

Yorkshire Post Newspapers: Madonna.

The Courtauld Institute of Art: John Wilson Carmichael's 'View of Waterloo Lake'.

Peter Brears: Drawing of William Nicholson Nicholson.

The Bodleian Library, University of Oxford: Huntsmen stalking stag: MS. Douce 336, fol.56.
Lopping trees: MS. Gough Liturg. 7, fol. 2r. Smiths working at a forge: MS. Bodley 264, pt.1. fol. 84.
Blacksmiths working an anvil: MS. Bodley 264, pt 1, fol.107.

Sheffield Industrial Museums Trust: Charcoal burning.

Leeds Museums and Galleries: Front cover: John Wilson Carmichael's ' View across to the Mansion'.

Leeds Library and Information Services: pp. 14, 18, 19, 20, 21, 30, 31, 34, 35, 37, 38, 39, 40, 41 and 42.

Leeds Library: 'The Graphic' p.16.

Front Cover:
Background Image - 'Roundhay Park in 1838' by John Wilson Carmichael (1800-1868). This is one of three watercolour paintings of the estate commissioned by Stephen Nicholson. Carmichael was born in Newcastle upon Tyne. After a period at sea and an apprenticeship to a shipbuilder, Carmichael became a pupil of the elder T. M. Richardson. He painted first in oils and then mostly in watercolour. He specialised in marine subjects. From 1838 he regularly sent paintings for exhibition at the Royal Academy.

Back cover:
'The Battlements of the Ruins of Roundhay Park' by Atkinson Grimshaw (1878). Private Collection, United Kingdom Courtesy of The Richard Green Gallery, London.
Huntsmen stalking stag: MS. Douce 336, fol.56. The Bodleian Library, University of Oxford.

WATERLOO LAKE AND PARK, ROUNDHAY.
AS SEEN FROM THE CASTLE

The Friends of Roundhay Park exists to ensure the continued preservation, restoration, maintenance and improvement of the Park for all its users and for future generations.

If you would like to join the Friends and can help or support us in any way then please write to:

The Membership Secretariat
5 Lakeview Court
Leeds LS8 2TX

e-mail for all enquiries: info@forp.co.uk

Tour the park in virtual reality: www.forp.co.uk